CONTENTS

SUSTAINING CITIES

New Directions in International Studies

Patrice Petro, Series Editor

The New Directions in International Studies series focuses on transculturalism, technology, media, and representation, and features the innovative work of scholars who explore various components and consequences of globalization, such as the increasing flow of peoples, ideas, images, information, and capital across borders. Under the direction of Patrice Petro, the series is sponsored by the Center for International Education at the University of Wisconsin–Milwaukee. The center seeks to foster interdisciplinary and collaborative research that probes the political, economic, artistic, and social processes and practices of our time.

SUSTAINING CITIES

Urban Policies, Practices, and Perceptions

EDITED BY
LINDA KRAUSE

RUTGERS UNIVERSITY PRESS
NEW BRUNSWICK, NEW JERSEY, AND LONDON

Library of Congress Cataloging-in-Publication Data

Sustaining cities : urban policies, practices, and perceptions / edited by
Linda Krause.
    p. cm. — (New directions in international studies)
    Includes bibliographical references and index.
    ISBN 978–0–8135–5416–7 (hardcover : alk. paper) — ISBN 978–0–8135–5415–0
(pbk. : alk. paper) — ISBN 978–0–8135–5417–4 (e-book)
    1. City planning—Environmental aspects.   2. Cities and town—Growth.
3. Sociology, Urban.   I. Krause, Linda.
    HT166.S9136   2013
    307.1′216—dc23

                                                                    2012005046

A British Cataloging-in-Publication record for this book is available from the
British Library.

Visit our website: http://rutgerspress.rutgers.edu

Manufactured in the United States of America

ACKNOWLEDGMENTS

This volume would not have been possible without the support and encouragement of many individuals. In April 2009 Patrice Petro and I organized an international conference, "Sustaining Cities: Urban Lost and Found," which was held at the University of Wisconsin–Milwaukee (UWM). The essays in this volume evolved from papers delivered at the conference. For their conference assistance, I am grateful to staff members at the Center for International Education and the School of Architecture and Urban Planning, UWM. Particularly helpful were Sara Tully, Tracy Buss, Tom McGuire, and Dennis Manley.

I am also indebted to Patrice Petro, in her role as series editor of New Directions in International Studies, for editorial guidance. John Boly, at Marquette University, provided advice and support at critical junctures in the editorial process. Leslie Mitchner and Lisa Boyajian at Rutgers University Press have proved invaluable. I am especially grateful to Paula Friedman for her help in preparing the final manuscript.

The School of Architecture and Urban Planning, particularly its dean, Robert Greenstreet, have provided generous support both for the conference and for this volume.

SUSTAINING CITIES

INTRODUCTION

Linda Krause

In one of my favorite Gary Larson cartoons, a distant mushroom cloud looms and cars jam the street as people flee the conflagration. Unfazed, a dog focuses on what's in front of his nose. "And then Jake saw something that captured his attention."[1] From my experience with selectively attentive canines, this rings true. And it is also true for the many human Jakes for whom urban matters are at best peripheral. But this human inattention is changing. Now that cities are facing the combined disasters of failing infrastructure, devalued housing, and high unemployment, the question arises: how can cities survive? *Sustaining Cities* offers a collection of essays that focus our attention on current urban problems while suggesting how they can be solved. And the essays reveal how urban planners, architects, novelists, and filmmakers tap the unique and complex character of cities in these tumultuous times.

In 2003, the *Global Cities* volume in this series examined globalization's effect on cinema, architecture and urbanism.[2] *Sustaining Cities* likewise views cities through a multidisciplinary lens. The intervening years have provided a lengthened perspective with which to judge the impact of global phenomena. Here, the essays are grouped in sections covering urban policies, practices, and perceptions, respectively, yet the volume encourages readers to create new cross-disciplinary connections. Indeed, forging new links—among urban stakeholders, as well as between citizens and their communities—is a recurrent theme.

The volume begins with urban policy, in a section titled Market Rules. As explored in these essays, this title refers both to the dominant role of supply-side economics and to the specific ways in which markets are manipulated.

In "Sustainable City: Crisis and Opportunity in Mexico," urban and regional planner Alfonso Iracheta places urban planning policy (and the lack thereof) in the context of sustainability. He sees the Northern Hemisphere's opposition of development versus sustainability as a false dichotomy. Iracheta notes that, in wealthier nations, public policy often seeks to modify development through programs supporting sustainable growth; in poorer countries, by contrast, public policy encourages insufficient and badly conceived development that creates environmental problems. Further, the concept of sustainability must be understood in a broader context, one that encompasses energy conservation, socio-spatial equality, integrated land-use strategies, and participatory governance. Where social actors once sought less government and more market, they are now looking for policy changes, broader involvement of all stakeholders, and policies rooted in current local conditions and issues. Toward the close of the essay, Iracheta's "New Principles for Urban Planning and Governance in Mexico" offers a path to a more equitable and sustainable urbanism.

If such equitable and sustainable urbanism is the goal, then public policy in American cities also deserves scrutiny. In her essay "Hostage Cities: Unsustainable Competition for Corporate Investment," urban studies theorist Linda McCarthy reveals how communities have entered into an unhealthy competition to attract corporations to their towns and cities. What may have begun as investment incentive programs to aid stricken cities by giving corporations preferential tax treatment in return for jobs has become at best a zero-sum game, at worst a shakedown. In a competitive global economy, cities must court national and multinational companies, but the contest is often rigged. McCarthy shows how local politicians support unquestioned (and unquestionable) assumptions about corporate investment, and are themselves implicated in the continuation of unsustainable economic policies. Indeed, even if unsuccessful in their bids to attract new investment, local politicians and developers often benefit from the competition for corporate investment. Using case studies from the Milwaukee area, McCarthy traces the intricate maneuvers used to lure corporate support. These tactics and lessons apply to hard-pressed urban areas throughout the country. U.S. municipalities, unlike European ones, have greater autonomy and can determine local investment and tax policy, but this autonomy, McCarthy notes, comes at a price. With no federal or supranational authority to intervene in the community's interest, cities are at the mercy of the corporations. And, as globalization has been defined in part as "a process driven by the logic of corporate profitability,"[3] it may be questioned whether what's good for GE is in fact good for municipalities.

While rust-belt Milwaukee labors to attract investment, sun-belt Phoenix basks in it. At least, until the 2008–2009 economic meltdown. Phoenix and other fast-growing cities felt particular pain when hyperdevelopment, especially in the housing market, collapsed. Some lay the blame at questionable lending practices and overextended borrowers, but housing scholar Sherry Ahrentzen urges considering the burst housing bubble in a larger context. In "Reframing Housing Value," Ahrentzen argues that the kind of market-driven housing development that Phoenix and other cities experience has its basis in seldom-examined practices and policies surrounding homeownership. For instance, ever-expanding suburbs,

which draw vital resources from cities, are not sustainable, yet, federal, state, and local regulations often thwart creative approaches to
housing. Like McCarthy, Ahrentzen notes that European planning
policies offer more sustainable housing alternatives, some of which
are being introduced into the United States. More attention should
be paid to housing, Ahrentzen argues, for it is not incidental to, but
at the root of, other urban issues. By reframing housing values, it is
possible to develop social, economic, and environmental policies
that support vibrant, diverse cities.

Connecting Communities, the second section of the volume, considers urban design and planning practice. As Iracheta noted, the
forging of new links often means rejecting old binaries, and this
rejection is a signal feature of the landscape urbanism movement.
Landscape architect Charles Waldheim, a contributor to this volume, coined the term "landscape urbanism" in the mid-1990s, and
the movement is associated with such prominent landscape architects, architects, and urbanists as James Corner, Grahame Shane,
Alex Krieger, and Elizabeth Diller.[4] Well-known examples include
the High Line in New York and the recently opened Madrid Rio.
With its focus on networks of communication, information, people,
and transportation, the relatively recent discipline of landscape
urbanism offers interesting parallels to globalization. Both assume
the existence of a global environment in which space, time, and matter overlap and intersect. Yet where globalization often produces a
disconnected and inchoate environment, landscape urbanism promises one that is interconnected and multivalent. Landscape urbanists
see the city not as a series of isolated landmarks but as a multilayered
topography. The networks that inhabit this terrain must be better
connected as the old binaries—vertical versus horizontal, developed
versus undeveloped, city versus suburb—become increasingly and
intentionally blurred. Rather than replicate the anonymous, globalized

city, landscape urbanism respects the specific physical, historic, and cultural characteristics associated with a given site, confirming and sustaining the local within a global context.

In his essay "Notes toward a History of Agrarian Urbanism," Waldheim asserts that the customary division between urban and rural is no longer relevant. Partly to accommodate the locavore and slow-food movement, partly to salvage contaminated brownfields, cities now encourage urban farming; farmlands are also being reclaimed from sprawling exurban developments. But, in these instances, agriculture is viewed as an afterthought—something plugged into the abused and abandoned spaces of the city and its surroundings. Waldheim argues for a new synthesis of urban and agrarian, one in which the two are interrelated and seamless. His precedents are three twentieth-century urban design proposals: Frank Lloyd Wright's "Broadacre City" (1934–1935), Ludwig Hilberseimer's "New Regional Pattern" (1945–1949), and Andrea Branzi's "Agronica" (1993–1994). Not only do these proposals alter misconceptions about the boundaries between urban and rural, but they also encourage new thinking about urban form. The city now might be considered not merely in the vertical axis of its buildings but also in the horizontal axis of its landscape. It might be seen not merely in terms of industrial production, but also in terms of agricultural means of production. Waldheim, in examining these urban agrarian proposals, is not suggesting replacement of lost urban factories with factory farming. Rather, he asks that people view agriculture— necessarily responsive to nature, climate, and terrain—as both a guide and a metaphor for creating an interconnected and vital urban landscape.

Until recently Angell Town, in the Brixton area of London, was neither vital nor interconnected. Rather, it was the poster child for all that was wrong with top-down neighborhood development. Back in the 1970s, its new council housing units were heralded as modern and efficient. Built in the heyday of Brutalism,[5] a popular architectural movement characterized by raw concrete megastructures, Angell Town's housing was clearly responding to well-intentioned planning and architectural solutions. But by the 1990s it had long represented a dreary, disconnected, *Clockwork Orange* backdrop. What an earlier generation of architects and urban planners misunderstood or simply ignored was the need to create meaningful and sustainable communities, as opposed to mere shelter. Urban planner Georgia Butina Watson, in her essay "The Art of Place-Making," first analyzes what went wrong and then offers "best practices" for making memorable, distinct, safe, and lively neighborhoods. Angell Town provides the lens through which Watson reveals new and important connections between dedicated professionals and concerned residents, old and new neighborhoods, historic and contemporary architectural design, public and private spaces, native and immigrant residents, and even parents and children. Neither a globalized non-place nor a Disneyfied small town, Angell Town has a unique and meaningful identity. That identify is not transferable, but the methods used to discover it are.

Like London, Boston is also known for its richly diverse neighborhoods. Located at the intersection of three of them, Mission Hill, Fenway/Kenmore, and South End, is Northeastern University (NEU). Architect Mo Zell, in her contribution to this volume, "Beyond Boundaries," describes the task she and partner Marc Roehrle faced when commissioned to design a memorial dedicated to NEU alumni who died in military service. In her essay, Zell reveals how an unprepossessing parcel of land became the site both of the new memorial and of urban connections at many scales and dimensions. Exploring their award-winning design reveals the intricate examination of site, space, materials, and users that combines

Waldheim's multilayered approach to the city with Watson's sensitivity to identity and place-making. By looking beyond conventional notions of boundary, Zell and Roehrle created a memorial that encourages participation at a variety of scales, from the intimate encounter with a soldier's name to the pathways connecting the site to the campus, neighborhoods, and city beyond.

Google *rust-belt* and you'll see a map of the United States with a large red swath from the Northeast to the upper Midwest. The same process might be repeated with the terms *sun-belt* or *Asian Tigers.* Such inclusive words speak to boom-and-bust market trends over wide areas. Open the map's street view, however, and there emerge some surprising site-specific responses to globalization and its aftermath. In *Tigers, Tricksters, and Other Urban Legends,* this volume's final section, the authors offer a close-up view of the global-local intersection as perceived by novelists and filmmakers.

With its rapid market upswings and downturns and instantly transferred complex financial transactions, globalization thrives in dynamic societies. This is most strikingly the case in contemporary China, where film and urban studies theorist Ackbar Abbas charts a frenetic, globalized urban identity. In the first part of his essay, "Chinese Cities: Design and Disappearance," Abbas characterizes the Chinese city in six ways: operatic, anticipatory, manic-depressive, arbitrage, entrepreneurial, and disappearing. Using these categories, he shows how the city is mutable and optimistic, yet riding on unfounded expectations. Thus Chinese cities display a schizophrenic character, at once exhilarating and, especially in the wake of the financial crisis, insecure. The six aspects that Abbas names are then traced in contemporary Chinese film. Abbas argues that film does not create a virtual city. Instead, the virtual city of contemporary China creates films: cinematic images of the city and the lives inhabiting it reveal the same confused and conflicted identity as the city itself. In the final section of his essay, Abbas analyzes how China has used the prized edifices of star architects to announce its emergence as a first-world culture and to predict its domination of the twenty-first century. Yet these iconic buildings, he notes, disconnect citizens from their cities, as well as the cities, with their rich history and culture, from their citizens. To address this issue, Abbas calls for design more attentive to the city's multiple layers and identities.

The refrain in Yeats's poem "September 1913" offers a poignant assessment:

> Romantic Ireland's dead and gone,
> It's with O'Leary in the grave.[6]

For Yeats the romantic Ireland of Georgian portals and forty shades of pastoral green was already lost a century ago. However, during the Celtic Tiger's roaring 1990s, Irish tourism cultivated not only traditional myths but some new ones; for a brief time, Ireland's robust economy, fueled by European Union investment and high-tech entrepreneurs, lured expatriates and other celtophiles with the promise of an authentic yet newly chic homeland.[7] Paralleling this carefully crafted narrative, however, is a less upbeat portrayal of society—one offered by mass market crime fiction set in urban Ireland. In his essay "From 'The Dead' to the Dead: The Disposable Bodies and Disposable Culture of Celtic Tiger Noir," literary critic Andrew Kincaid reveals how Irish detective novels mirror the broad and deep changes brought about by both the rise and collapse of Ireland's economy. According to Kincaid, the noir detective novel, with its urban milieu and fast-paced writing style, is itself a reflection of recent changes in Ireland; during its recent burst of economic growth, Ireland became an increasingly urban and fast-paced society, Kincaid argues, but, now that the economy has failed, the noir subject matter, which often focuses on urban despair, excoriates Ireland's arrogance-laced boom while prowling its disillusion-fed bust.

The flip side of Kincaid's world-weary gumshoes might be found in Harlem's canny gangsters. Film studies theorist Paula Massood, in her contribution titled "Imagining and Reimagining a Promised Land: The Gangster Genre and Harlem's Mythic Past, Present, and Future," traces the cinematic presentation of the Harlem gangster from its beginnings in the 1930s to Denzel Washington's turn in *American Gangster* (2007). Like the Irish detective novel, the gangster film genre is a quintessentially urban form. In this case, moreover, it is set in a very specific urban milieu. Massood's essay considers how the films capture and promote images of the community both in the way Harlem residents see themselves and in the way filmmakers want their community to be seen by others. From the mythic Harlem Renaissance of the 1920s and 1930s through the gritty *Superfly* era of the 1970s to the present, increasingly upscale, neighborhood, each reframing of Harlem offers a new identity and a new myth. Replacing the 1930s urban trickster—a valued member and protector of Harlem—is today's global gangster, who, like some transnational corporation, has little nostalgia for the old neighborhood. To the degree with which Harlem residents identify with the cinematic gangsters (and Massood suggests that this historically has been the case), perhaps even mythic Harlem, in all its guises, has already disappeared.[8]

Cities change in response to economic, environmental, social, and political vicissitudes. To several of the authors, notably Iracheta, Ahrentzen, and McCarthy, such changes have been more regressive than progressive. These writers argue that short-sighted policies have led to unsustainable—even uninhabitable—cities. Even once-lauded and well-intentioned policies, as Watson shows, no longer work. For Waldheim, alternatives to such failed policies may require a paradigm shift, but for Zell, alternatives may simply require a more attentive look at what is unique about a locality. Contributors Kincaid, Massood, and Abbas explore urban change as presented in contemporary novels and films. These arts, beyond reflecting the altered urban milieu, are themselves products of it. What the essays in this volume share is the sense that we are at a fork in the road. They tell us what has happened and offer directions on the path to sustaining cities.

NOTES

1. Gary Larson, *The Far Side Gallery 2* (Kansas City, Mo.: Universal Press Syndicate, 1984), 181.

2. Linda Krause and Patrice Petro, eds., *Global Cities: Cinema, Architecture, and Urbanism in a Digital Age* (New Brunswick, N.J.: Rutgers University Press, 2003).

3. Walden Bello, *Deglobalization: Ideas for a New World Economy,* new ed. (London and New York: Zed Books, 2004), xii.

4. For views from several practitioners, see Charles Waldheim, ed., *The Landscape Urbanism Reader* (Princeton, N.J.: Princeton Architectural Press, 2006).

5. Brutalism derived its name from the *béton brut,* or raw, reinforced concrete, that was characteristic of Le Corbusier's post–World War II architecture. The term was introduced by British architects Peter and Alison Smithson. During the 1970s, Brutalist buildings appeared in all industrialized nations.

6. William Butler Yeats, "September 1913," in *The Collected Poems of W. B. Yeats,* ed. Richard Finneran (New York: Scribner Paperback Poetry, 1996), 108–109.

7. Ireland's successful attempt to attract and retain artists predates the recent economic boom. In 1969, then minister of finance Charles Haughey introduced measures that exempted artists from paying income tax on sales of their work. Ireland also offered generous incentives for business investment, especially in the area of research and development. Such strategies were in place decades before Richard Florida, in *Cities and the Creative Class* (New York: Routledge, 2005), claimed that cities which welcomed creative artists and entrepreneurs thrived, while those that did not failed. Yet, as Ireland has demonstrated, even creative and innovative environments are not recession-proof.

8. Massood notes that, in the opening scene of *American Gangster,* an elderly crime boss regrets the arrival of a big-box electronics store. One can imagine his reaction to the news that in 2010 Manhattan's first Target store had opened in Harlem. For more on this event see Stephanie Clifford, "The Fruits of Target's Wooing," *New York Times,* August 14, 2010, Business Day-1.

PART I

URBAN POLICIES

MARKET RULES

SUSTAINABLE CITY

CRISIS AND OPPORTUNITY
IN MEXICO

Alfonso Iracheta

A Theoretical Note

During the last two or three decades, urban theories mainly have been directed toward analyzing the impact globalization has had in the territory being studied, and highlighting issues of squatter settlements, urban poverty, and environmental deterioration. As has been stressed by UN-HABITAT, new forces driving worldwide human settlements call for reconsideration by both society and government of how urban policy and planning are conducted.[1] Regions and cities are facing such complex phenomena as: hyper-urbanization, poverty concentration, land-use disorder, climate change, cultural clashes, and migration. Typically these phenomena are analyzed from a mainstream perspective strongly oriented toward the relationship between globalization and economic restructuring and space. In these approaches, urban space is regarded as a "thing in itself," as something given with an existence independent of matter.

Further, most spatial analysis consists of the sum of constraints, whether they be the geographical-environmental features, the inherited built environment, the lack of public or private investment, the inappropriate legislation and territorial administration (in regions or cities), or the institutional responses through public policy and planning. Víctor Ramiro Fernández (like others) criticizes this spatial current of thought, which he calls the "new regionalist orthodoxy," as an academic effort concentrated in industrialized societies, supported by national governments and multilateral organizations, that has been strong enough to influence the creation of new institutions and public policies and practices.[2] This approach has been imported by underdeveloped countries, giving rise to local versions that, in turn, have resulted in new spatial and environmental public policies and institutions. Thus, as has been recognized by the most important Latin American analysts working in the field of urban and regional spatial research, after three decades of national and international efforts, compared to intellectual production in the so-called central countries, indigenous solutions have been rather scarce. What is lacking is a more comprehensive concept and a more critical theoretical position regarding what has been called the "capitalist city." It is not a question of scholars wanting to return to old theories, which might imply a return to 1970s neo-Marxism, but rather of critically revisiting contemporary urban development and sustainability.

THE SUSTAINABLE CITY PROBLEM IN MEXICO

I begin with two hypotheses: Mexican cities as now constituted are unsustainable; and, the problem of urban sustainability has not been adequately formulated by the Mexican government or society. Within the dominant development model in Mexico, there are in place public policies to address not only environmental sustainability, but also many other problems related to the development process. However, proposed solutions do not reflect the sustainable city problem per se but rather the dominant interests of capital accumulation. This is why urban and environmental planning and public policy in Mexico have not even achieved the positive results possible within this economic-political model in the developed world.

The essence of Mexico's sustainable city crisis is, first of all, a social crisis. In this crisis, social actors struggle to appropriate space, and they view the environment as an object and commodity. The commodification of the natural world reinforces the tendency to divorce urban sustainable development from social struggles: sustainability is seen as *something else.* Mexico's sustainable city problem also has to be understood as a confrontation between two different perspectives: that of economic development and that of environmental sustainability. Analysts agree that in most Latin American countries, since the early 1980s, economic growth has increased, whereas social and environmental sustainability has decreased or stagnated.[3] In developed countries, there is a growing tendency to view economic growth and environmental policies as mutually compatible and noncontradictory[4] to such an extent that the latter becomes an important incentive for the former.[5] But in less developed countries environmental problems are mainly a consequence of poverty and underdevelopment. Poverty reduces people's capability to use natural resources in a sustainable fashion, thereby intensifying pressure on the environment.[6] Poor people are forced to forgo future needs to meet those of the present.[7] Therefore, what concerns the countries of the South—poverty, inequality, potable water, land desertification, and the like—are problems profoundly different from those besetting the countries of the North.[8]

Even though economic and political interests are at stake, a country like Mexico is debating environmental and urban public policies with almost no success in defining sustainable cities' development priorities. To understand this crisis, we must begin with a discussion of the unfair, unbalanced relationship between society and the natural environment that has been imposed by Mexico's dominant model of development.[9]

CRITICAL ENVIRONMENTAL PROBLEMS
IN MEXICAN CITIES

Natural resource destruction and misuse, along with the systematic violence wielded against the environment in many Mexican cities, justify a search for new ways of thought that allow us to resolve the irrationality of the economic-political development model. The more significant problems in cities and metropolises include, inter alia: low productivity and competitiveness, poverty and inequality, chaotic land use, poor mobility, environmental deterioration, lax governance, and misguided economic policies.

National and regional development depends greatly on cities, especially on more populated ones such as the Mexico City Metropolitan Area (MCMA), which accounts for over 30 percent of the GNP, with less than 20 percent of the country's population. As has been recorded since the early 1990s by the *Fideicomiso de Estudios Estratégicos sobre la Ciudad de México* (Mexico City's Strategic Study Trust), the MCMA's productivity is declining.[10] The reasons are higher transaction costs and negative effects caused by land-use disorder, lower mobility, and increasing land, water, and air pollution. All these problems directly affect the productivity and global competitiveness of Mexico's national capital—none more so than poverty and socioeconomic inequality.

Depending on the source, between 50 and 70 percent of Mexico's urban population is poor.[11] It is not only that poverty is increasingly concentrated in cities and metropolises, but that the economic crisis is reducing the number of formal jobs, so that about 60 percent of new urban jobs are in the informal sector; further, as the Mexican economy becomes increasingly global, the distribution of wealth becomes less equitable. The result is larger urban populations of low- and very low-income workers. And these workers place greater demands on housing, infrastructure, services, and the environment.

Mexican cities have been growing since the early 1950s without solving the issues of an adequate urban form and land-use distribution. There are also land speculation and land tenure irregularities. That is why the last five decades have been called the period of wild urbanization. When new housing policies were developed at the turn of the millennium, their main objective was to offer as many houses as possible without regard for social and environmental issues. The consequence is that, after nearly a decade of more than half a million new houses annually, most of the construction has contributed virtually nothing to orderly urban growth. On the contrary, many cities are expanding so widely that they have thousands of empty hectares within the city limits and the immediate periphery, and are at risk of having a permanently chaotic urban pattern. Add the extent of poorly constructed, irregular, and precarious human settlements on the outskirts of most cities, and the problem of urban sustainability and spatial ordering becomes paramount, and there are also issues of impeded vehicular and pedestrian mobility.

The number of vehicles in Mexico has been growing constantly; in 2003 there were approximately 21.2 million registered vehicles. Each year, there are around 1.16 million new motor vehicles, representing an annual growth rate of around 7.4 percent. In turn, the MCMA concentrates 25 percent of the nation's vehicles, with a total of 4.5 million vehicles in 2001. This number rose by approximately 300,000 annually between 1997 and 2001.[12] Since the early 1950s, Mexican policy concerning urban mobility has been, following the United States' and other countries' postwar strategy, clearly oriented toward promoting the use of private cars. However, on the one hand, most Mexican cities have a colonial road pattern unsuitable for a huge number of private cars, and, on the other hand, there are no clear public transport and other mobility strategies. The consequence is that cities are filled with cars, but they lack the appropriate pedestrian and bicycle infrastructure and functional, adequate public mass transport systems that would increase mobility for all inhabitants. Mexico City's Metropolitan Environmental Commission estimated that MCMA's traffic congestion has cost seven billion dollars (US) per year. As with land-use and urban structure policies, Mexican cities need an integrated mobility strategy. An adequate mass transit infrastructure would also help reduce automobile emissions.

Mexico's cities have contributed to the degradation of the environment, and have misused vital natural resources. From Central Mexico northward, almost all cities face a huge water shortage and, to some degree, water pollution, because water treatment and reuse are relatively recent policies and many cities have failed to meet deadlines proposed by the federal government. The problem of waste management is also behind schedule, and urban waste disposal has been subject to various modes of privatization rather than being managed as a public service under local government responsibility. As a result of such lacks and failures, many urban projects have failed during the past few years, leaving local society with environmental problems and local government without the necessary tools for solving such problems internally. Moreover, due to urban expansion, the existence of agricultural and forestry land in urban peripheries has become an environmental problem. Because the developer-dominated urbanization process typically is seen as a question of housing or other land-use supply mechanisms rather than as something to be approached in a holistic, community-oriented manner, the result is a disorganized and unsustainable urban structure at war with nature.

From a global perspective, the world is facing a revolution that started in the mid-1980s with the fall of the Berlin Wall. The principal consequences have been twofold: a new unipolar view of global politics offers a vision of free trade and market-driven national politics; at the same time, neoliberal economics cast aside many public policy traditions by transforming or even reducing citizens to consumers and recipients of government social services. Similarly, urban land has become primarily a real estate commodity, implying that those who can't afford land prices are expelled to the city's outskirts; in Mexico such persons constitute more than half the total urban population. The (relative) abandonment of urban and environmental planning by the Mexican government since the early 1980s has shown that, with certain exceptions, no tier of government (federal, state, or municipal) has sufficient political strength, technical skill, and resources to solve urban community needs, particularly those of the urban poor.

Beginning in the early 1980s, when economic and political neoliberalism was installed in Mexico, the federal government reduced its own resources, power, capabilities, and legitimacy, making way for the private sector to take over an important share of public decisions. Without any national debate, suddenly the market(s) became the leading agent in economic, and also in spatial and environmental, policies. With no clear rules of translation from the private to the public domain, new forms of planning and of public-policy design and decision making were put into practice.

As a result, community-based planning principles were rejected, and the market was left to decide, for instance, about the location of most infrastructure, housing, and other urban facilities. The 1992 constitutional amendment which gave birth to a new agrarian law paved the way for the privatization of *ejidal* land, which represents more than three quarters of urbanizable land in most Mexican cities. This ejidal land[13] was the natural social escape valve for the urban poor (more than 60 percent of urban informal settlements are located there). Once most *ejidatarios* could privatize their plots of land, prices began going up, to match average real estate prices, in each city. The consequence was an increase in the supply of peripheral urbanizable land, with the possibility of price reductions in favor of the formal land market and, paradoxically, a decrease in land supply for the urban poor, who have been forced to pay higher land prices or move to settlements farther from the city limits. The relative withdrawal of the government from spatial and environmental decision making—even though spatial and environmental planning have continued to exist—led to rampant land speculation; this has been one of the most important reasons why the urban poor have been expelled from the formal city. An estimated three million families now live in informal settlements. These people cannot afford a plot of land and other, associated costs (urban services, land taxes, and the like),[14] so they must reside in environmentally unsound and remote areas.

All these problems have exacerbated a breakdown in social arrangements and reduced local governance capabilities. Increasingly, employment, housing, transit, and public services tend to be informal in the poorest areas of cities. The social actors who pleaded in the late 1970s for much more market, and less state, intervention and planning are now asking for strong government intervention in critical urban matters.

New Principles for Urban Planning
and Governance in Mexico

Any conceptual contribution toward understanding sustainability and transforming Mexico's urban development should address some essential ideas: energy conservation, socio-spatial equality, integrated land-use strategies, and participatory governance. Public policy strategies for addressing urban problems should consider how to direct resources to poorer and less educated inhabitants within cities and metropolises. From this standpoint, it is important to realize that urban informal settlements and informal markets, although constituting a huge social and environmental problem, have also served as a sort of solution both because they have evidenced an ability to offer housing suited to the income constraints of the urban poor and because they have diminished urban social unrest. What informal housing solutions lack is land tenure and housing certainty; thus, a transformation of Mexico's urban land regularization strategy is needed. In addition, academic and social working groups of the National Housing Council have amply demonstrated that the promotion of, and incentives for, mass supply of serviced land suitable for the urban poor (in price, location, basic services, and terms of payment) must be features of the national strategies if the government and society are to be truly committed to reducing urban inequality and poverty. There should also be public support for self-building and socially concerned housing production: until now, housing policy has been solely directed to the less poor of the poor and has not improved urban-metropolitan sustainability. Finally, Mexico needs a national urban-metropolitan land policy that requires certification of property rights and compliance with land obligations.

Mexican cities need a national, sustainable urban mobility policy that would be oriented to the long term, be integrated with urban development, and be widely participatory. The aims of this policy should be to promote sustainable urban mobility as a civil right, and to integrate mobility strategies with those of urban planning, environmental protection, and public health. Other objectives should be to reduce the number of cars within cities by offering high-quality public transport (mainly bus, rapid transit, light rail, and nonmotorized means of transport), as well as by mandating fuel-efficient cars and buses.

The search for sustainable cities in Mexico calls for new principles based on a different form of government, through which citizens and social actors can collectively solve their problems and attend to their social needs, using government as the main instrument to attain their goals. This new government is called governance (*gobernanza*). In some Latin American countries, and particularly in Mexico, governance is a new sociopolitical model that places greater value on the local social resources and capabilities of a territory and encourages politics to go beyond public administration and political parties to include social actors and their organizations, as well. As a consequence, representative and participatory democracy is a fundamental principle of governance, and the source of citizenship building. This requires greater co-responsibility in urban policy decisions between the government and social actors, all of which necessarily involves a reevaluation of politics and the creation of a new relationship between government and society. For governance to work it must distinguish between public and private spheres, rebuild social networks, view urbanization as a socio-spatial construct, encourage participant diversity, and be sensitive to local concerns.

A Closing Note

I remember from my days as a very young scholar in the early 1970s how the urban-metropolitan sustainability crisis was envisioned through many research projects and the methods we used to alert the government about the magnitude of the risks that Mexican society was to face. Many intelligent, deeply committed civil servants from federal and state governments shared this vision and supported the proposals that emerged from it. Regrettably, all of this was virtually lost when urban space and the environment became a mere commodity to be dealt with by the market with practically no government intervention.

Now, the limitation to seriously confronting the unsustainable city problem in Mexico is not merely loss of momentum. Rather, due to nearly thirty years of market dominance in this sphere, and little government effort to order and control urbanization processes, the issue has become a very low priority. There is a real risk that it will no longer be possible to solve many urban sustainability problems and that many others may follow similar paths downward. For all these reasons, Mexicans should resolve to *politicize urban space and the environment* in the sense of putting both at the highest level of the national political debate. The time has come to make cities and sustainability mutually compatible and of very high priority.

ACKNOWLEDGMENTS

The author wishes to thank Susan Beth Kapilian for her careful editorial revision of the text.

NOTES

1. *Planning Sustainable Cities: Policy Directions: Global Report on Human Settlements, 2009*, United Nations Human Settlements Programme (London: Earthscan, 2009), *passim*.

2. Víctor Ramiro Fernández, Ash Amin, and José Ignacio Vigil, compilers, *Repensando el desarrollo regional: Contribuciones globales para una estrategia latinoamericana* (Buenos Aires: Miño y Dávila Editores, 2008), 19.

3. Víctor Ramiro Fernández and Sergio Boisier, *El vuelo de una cometa: Una metáfora para una teoría del desarrollo territorial* (Santiago de Chile: Instituto Latinoamericano de Planificación Económica y Social, 1997), 558.

4. David Pearce et al., *Blueprint for a Green Economy* (London: Earthscan, 1989), *passim*. See also Michael Jacobs, *The Green Economy: Environment, Sustainable Development, and the Politics of the Future* (London: Pluto Press, 1991), *passim*.

5. Andrew Blowers, "Environmental Policy: The Quest for Sustainable Development," *Urban Studies* 30, no. 4/5 (1993): 775–796.

6. Brundtland Commission, *The Brundtland Report, Our Common Future*, World Commission on Environment and Development (Oxford: Oxford University Press, 1987), 49.

7. Johan Holmberg et al., *Defending the Future: A Guide to Sustainable Development* (London: IIED/Earthscan, 1991), 32.

8. Blowers, "Environmental Policy": 779.

9. Eduardo Galeano, "Naturaleza muerta," *La Jornada*, April 10, 1995, 20.

10. *Fideicomiso de Estudios Estratégicos sobre la Ciudad de México*, "La Ciudad de México hoy, bases para un diagnóstico" (Mexico: Gobierno del Distrito Federal, 2000).

11. CONEVAL, "Reporta CONEVAL cifras de pobreza por ingreso 2008," press release no. 006/09, July 18, 2009. See also Julio Boltvinik and Araceli Damián, coordinators, *La pobreza en México y el mundo: Realidades y desafíos* (Mexico: Siglo XXI Editores, 2004), 541.

12. Alfonso Iracheta, *La necesidad de una política pública para el desarrollo de sistemas integrados de transporte en grandes ciudades mexicanas*, INE, Centro Mario Molina, CTS (Zinacantepec, Mexico: El Colegio Mexiquense, 2006), 14–16, 48.

13. An *ejido* is a form of "social" land tenure that has existed in Mexico since the pre-Hispanic era. It was modernized after the 1910–1920 agrarian revolution giving birth to an agrarian reform, through which around one million hectares were distributed among peasants, who became *ejidatarios*, and their community land, ejidos. The new Agrarian Law of 1992 represented the end of agrarian reform and the beginning of ejido privatization.

14. Alfonso Iracheta and Martim Smolka, "Access to Serviced Land for the Urban Poor: The Regularization Paradox in Mexico," *Economía, Sociedad y Territorio*, 2, no. 8 (Zinacantepec, Mexico: El Colegio Mexiquense, 2000), 757–789.

HOSTAGE CITIES

UNSUSTAINABLE COMPETITION FOR CORPORATE INVESTMENT

Linda McCarthy

Newspaper reports like the following are increasingly common across the United States:

> In a move that is sure to set off a bidding war among communities in southeast Wisconsin and other states, Astronautics Corp. of America, a low-key but high-tech Milwaukee manufacturer, is seeking a new headquarters site that would employ 1,000 people.... Astronautics has retained Steve Palec, senior vice president of CB Richard Ellis in Milwaukee, to conduct the search. Palec was involved in 2007 in procuring headquarters for GE Healthcare in Wauwatosa and Manpower Inc. in Milwaukee.... While Astronautics executives prefer to remain in Milwaukee, CB Richard Ellis will conduct a national search, Palec said. "There's nothing that would not be on the table right now."
>
> Dozens of southeast Wisconsin developers and communities have entered the derby to win what could be the Milwaukee area's biggest economic development deal in these recessionary times: a new headquarters for Astronautics.... The 50-year-old

company has made it clear that a major factor in determining its new location will be incentives. . . . The company sought submissions that include development zones, low-interest loans and grants, infrastructure assistance, and "lowered acquisition or occupancy costs," according to its request for proposals. . . . It's likely the company is seeking financial incentives comparable to those the city of Milwaukee offered to lure Manpower Inc.'s headquarters and the city of Wauwatosa offered to attract GE Healthcare.[1]

In a global economy, competition using public incentives to attract nationally or internationally mobile companies has intensified to the point where a culture of competition now pervades state and local government economic development policy and spending.

Upping the ante are major employers like Manpower, GE Healthcare, and Astronautics that can threaten to relocate and then play places against each other. The winning locality gets the company, certainly, but the competitive pressures hike up the price of success—obligatory tax breaks, of course, but also expensive public outlays like grants and subsidized land parcels. When the incentives merely involve relocations within the same metropolitan region, the company may not even create any new jobs or investment.

Within the context of sustaining cities, no one is arguing that incentives to encourage economic development are a bad or irrational use of public funds. Some incentives may benefit cities, such as tax breaks to attract a foreign corporation, grants for new start-up enterprises, or infrastructure investments to encourage a company to expand in an economically distressed neighborhood. But others may be wasteful subsidies for cities, if they are zero sum at a metropolitan, state, or national scale.

STATE AND LOCAL GOVERNMENT COMPETITION
FOR CORPORATE INVESTMENT

During the last few decades, state and local governments have increased their business incentive programs in an effort to retain or attract company investment and jobs.[2] These programs usually entail corporate subsidies involving foregone public revenues, such as tax credits for companies, and government expenditures involving upfront public spending, like grants to companies or upgraded urban infrastructure, usually paid for through tax increment financing (TIF).

In TIF, a municipality sets aside the difference between pre- and post-redevelopment property taxes (the increment) to pay off the often millions of dollars in TIF bonds that are sold to help finance the redevelopment in the first place. Although using the future tax increment to help pay for a redevelopment sounds attractive, drawbacks include loss of tax base due to unnecessary TIF use in areas where redevelopment would have occurred anyway, and a lack of transparency because, not being general obligation bonds, TIF bonds do not require voter approval.

In their desperate desire for economic development, government agencies increasingly negotiate with companies for their investment. Fueling this culture of competition are government officials who face increasing pressures to win corporate investment and generate tangible results such as new jobs for their jurisdiction. The result, as captured by one particularly well-titled academic journal article, is that government officials are prone to "shoot anything that flies; claim anything that falls."[3]

There are no accurate estimates, but the value of state and local incentives to businesses in the United States may have risen to as much as $50 billion annually.[4] States and localities argue that incentives are necessary to attract and retain business investment and jobs in a highly competitive global economy. They maintain that the public revenues generated by these private investments more than cover the cost of the incentives.

Box 1. GE Healthcare, Wauwatosa, Wisconsin

In 2002, GE Healthcare announced its intention to consolidate its metropolitan Milwaukee operations from Menomonee Falls, Milwaukee, and West Milwaukee into one site. The move involved relocating twelve hundred existing jobs, and the promise of about seven hundred new ones.

GE retained CB Richard Ellis as its site location consultant. The request for proposals (RFP) helped fuel a culture of competition among Milwaukee and neighboring communities who competed for the new facility. The finalists among the proposals included several incentive packages with sites in: the proposed twenty-two-story Ovation Plaza office building in downtown Milwaukee; the Pabst Farms development in Oconomowoc; and the Woodland Prime office complex in Menomonee Falls. In 2004, GE announced its decision to move immediately west of Milwaukee to a new building with free parking in the Milwaukee County Research Park in Wauwatosa. Irgens Development Company built the $89 million, 506,000 sq. ft. offices. GE Healthcare signed a twelve-year lease and moved into the building in 2006. The incentive package totaled about $36 million:

- $29 million from the City of Wauwatosa, comprising a $15 million grant to Irgens Development Company to help fund construction of a parking structure, combined with a $10 million low-interest loan (this $25 million was raised by selling TIF bonds); $2.7 million to purchase the land from Milwaukee County; and a $1.3 million moving allowance for GE.

- Over $7 million from the State of Wisconsin for GE, comprising $6.5 million in tax credits and a $510,000 forgivable loan (despite the fact that GE was not threatening to relocate from Wisconsin, having narrowed down its site choice to either Wauwatosa or Milwaukee in 2003).

Concerns about Wasteful Competition for Corporate Investment

The competition by state and local governments for corporate investment has numerous drawbacks. Enormous public resources can be diverted as incentives for private companies in the form of direct outlays like grants, or foregone as lost revenue, as with tax breaks. Provision of such incentivess can strain already tight government budgets, especially during severe economic downturns. Some instances have been documented of fewer gains in jobs and other economic benefits than initially projected; many more such instances go unnoticed due to lax monitoring, as, for example, the *Milwaukee Journal Sentinel* reported in 2007.

Wisconsin distributes millions of dollars of taxpayer money to companies each year to encourage economic growth and job creation. But the state fails to track subsidies to see whether they work. If officials did check, they'd find that thousands of new jobs promised by companies in exchange for state aid never materialized. The *Journal Sentinel* examined twenty companies that were awarded about $80 million in state subsidies over a six-year period, including the ten largest aid recipients. These twenty-five firms accounted for roughly one-fourth of all business subsidies given. Only two of the companies fully reported their job creation and retention efforts, causing huge gaps in the state's accounting. Where records were unavailable, the *Journal Sentinel* contacted the companies to find the accurate totals. Among the findings:

- About 40 percent of the jobs companies agreed to create for their subsidies do not currently exist.
- The state spent nearly $17,000 per new job, 70 percent more than the state's own guideline for an acceptable subsidy.
- When companies do report lower job totals, the state often adjusts its requirements for job creation downward rather than cancel subsidies or seek repayment.[5]

The distribution of the costs and benefits of governments competing for private investment can be inequitable if more of the tax burden is shifted to property owners and away from private companies, or if larger, more mobile companies are favored over smaller ones. Some studies have found that poorer cities pay more in incentives than do richer ones, with the costs outweighing the benefits for some poorer cities. In fact, quite a number of studies have concluded that public incentives do not always offset their cost.[6]

What is more, state and local governments that compete and do not win the company spend significant time and financial resources on each unsuccessful attempt. Because only one city can win, this competition is zero sum if it merely relocates investment between places at public expense.[7] If public funds are diverted from more productive investments, such as education, technology, and the transportation and communications infrastructures, the competing cities and states may become less competitive nationally and internationally.

Adding to concerns about wasteful competition are the surveys of company decision making that indicate that incentives may only primarily influence a company's decision about where to locate within a single metropolitan region. This is because companies usually narrow their choice to a particular metropolitan region on the basis of fundamental production requirements, such as the quality and cost of labor. Only then does the final site decision take into account public incentives. So for a metropolitan regional economy as a whole, there may be no overall benefit to offering incentives to encourage a company to locate in one locality rather than another within that metropolitan regional economy.[8]

Box 2. Manpower, Milwaukee, Wisconsin

In 2005, Manpower announced it was looking for a new headquarters, where it could consolidate its metropolitan Milwaukee (Glendale and Brookfield) operations. The move involved relocating nine hundred existing jobs, and the promise of about three hundred new ones. Manpower was the largest company to seek new offices in the Milwaukee metropolitan region since GE Healthcare.

Like GE, Manpower retained CB Richard Ellis as its site-location consultant. Manpower's RFP resulted in a list of nine communities with incentive offers. The finalists were Milwaukee, Wauwatosa, and Glendale. In this culture of competition, the contest over Manpower was intense: "We're ready to roll out the red carpet to assist the company with finding a new location that can best suit their needs" (Milwaukee mayor); "We are willing to do whatever we can to keep them" (Glendale city administrator).[*]

Later in 2005, Manpower announced its decision to move to a new building in downtown Milwaukee. Riverbend LLC, a group of investors led by local developer Gary Grunau, built the $63 million, 280,000 sq. ft. offices. Manpower signed a seventeen-year lease and moved into the building in 2007.

The incentive package from the City of Milwaukee totaled $28.36 million:

1. $20.6 million for the parking structure, which the city now owns and leases to Riverbend LLC with an option to purchase (one thousand free parking spaces were a requirement in Manpower's RFP);

2. a $1.7 million grant and a $3 million low-interest loan to Riverbend to help build the office building (the funds for Riverbend were raised through TIF bonds);

3. a $560,000 moving allowance for Manpower, plus $600,000 to cover Manpower's old lease holdover allowance;

4. $1.9 million in infrastructure improvements, including an extension of the Milwaukee Riverwalk.

*Pete Millard. "Powerhouse Tenant Hits Market," *The Business Journal* April 1, 2005. http://milwaukee.bizjournals.com/milwaukee/stories/2005/04/04/story1.html.

Addressing Wasteful Competition?

To the extent that some incentives are clearly wasteful, including those for companies that are merely threatening to leave a locality, the prospects for minimizing wasteful competition appear bleak. One reason is that, apart from being able to point to the potential economic benefits if the community "wins" the company, politicians and economic development officials enjoy the actual political benefits that come with groundbreaking and ribbon-cutting ceremonies. With the costs often unseen or borne later, and because it is not clear that incentives are always ineffective, offering such incentives has symbolic value: efforts to offer incentives can be pointed to even if a locality loses.[9]

Despite the fact that government officials generally agree that eliminating wasteful competition is rational, each local government can feel forced, acting individually, to offer incentives to companies, since there is no certainty that acting collectively the other localities will not do so. As a result, in the battle for investment, bottom-up solutions representing unilateral disarmament appear unlikely: most localities fear that, if they disarm, the available investment will go to those localities that continue to offer incentives.[10] Contributing to this prisoner's dilemma, potential investors avoid specifying the size of the incentive package necessary to secure their investment; this allows companies to play localities against each other to drive up the value of the incentive offers. Interstate noncompetition or anti-poaching pacts that have been attempted in the past have been weak and unstable; politicians change over time, and the multitude of incentives makes it too easy for an individual locality to defect.[11]

The option of offering only seemingly productive incentives, such as job training and infrastructure that remain in a community even if the company does not, may not be viable. If the prisoner's dilemma and the weak bargaining position of governments relative to businesses make states and localities unable to withhold incentives in the first place, they are even less likely to be able to dictate the kinds of incentives to be offered to the company.[12]

Metropolitan regional cooperation offers advantages in theory, but is difficult in practice. McCarthy investigated the potential for intergovernmental cooperation in the Toledo Jeep plant relocation.[13] Despite Chrysler's preference for building the new plant in the Toledo metropolitan region, thereby presenting opportunities for alternatives to wasteful competition, there were too many impediments. The main obstacle was that the Jeep plant represented the retention of a high-profile company for Toledo, which the city's mayor had vowed not to lose to an adjacent locality.

Some federal involvement may be needed, therefore, to address wasteful competition in a top-down manner. Congress could abolish the power of the states to grant incentives.[14] It could ban incentives that favor a particular company, allowing only incentives that apply to all companies that meet specified eligibility criteria. This would be difficult to enforce in practice, however, because states and localities could try to get around the ban in creative ways—for example, by manipulating their tax structures.

A federal tax on companies, equal to the value of the incentives, or a reduction in federal funding to states and localities by the same amount, would face similar enforcement problems; the vast array of incentives makes it difficult to establish which are general incentives applying to all companies and which are reserved for particular companies. The federal establishment of an across-the-board corporate state income tax level is unlikely. Many analysts see resistance within Congress to infringe upon the rights of states, as well as opposition, not only from states and localities but also from other interests, especially businesses, that benefit from the incentives.[15]

Box 3. Summit Place, West Allis, Wisconsin

In 2002, developer-landlord Whitnall Summit broke ground at the former Allis-Chalmers manufacturing facility in West Allis. The first phase of Summit Place opened in 2004. This 157-acre former brownfield is now a $50 million, 650,000 sq. ft. office complex.

The incentive package totaled $19.8 million:

1. $7.5 million in TIF from the City of West Allis toward the cost of the building infrastructure and to build a parking structure;
2. $12 million federal new market tax credits (to promote investment in distressed areas) from the State of Wisconsin's Housing and Economic Development Authority;
3. $300,000 brownfield cleanup grant from the State of Wisconsin's Department of Commerce.

Summit Place is just fourteen blocks west of Milwaukee, and offers free parking. The total number of jobs at the site is about two thousand, most of which are not new to the metropolitan region.

In 2006, Anthem (formerly Blue Cross Blue Shield) announced its relocation to Summit Place, taking 750 workers from downtown Milwaukee and another 40 from California. Within the culture of competition, the City of Milwaukee offered $1.6 million in incentives to entice the company to stay. Anthem turned down the offer because it expected to save $8 million over its ten-year lease of a 150,000 sq. ft. building in Summit Place (based on rents of $13.95 per sq. ft. in Summit Place versus $16.50 downtown).

Other Summit Place tenants and their new square footage include Alterra Healthcare, which relocated from the Milwaukee County Research Park in Wauwatosa (44,000 sq. ft.); Merge Technologies, which relocated from within West Allis (22,000 sq. ft.); Associated Equipment, Legal Placement Services, MCI, Poblocki Signs, Triad Engineering, and Wisconsin Dental Association, all relocating from Milwaukee (about 110,000 sq. ft. combined); and an expansion of the Sanford Brown College (35,000 sq. ft.).

Evaluating the Culture of Competition: The Case of Milwaukee, Wisconsin

No one is questioning that state and local governments need corporate investment, but the Milwaukee examples (see boxes 1–3) raise the question: at what cost? An individual locality may secure new jobs, but these jobs can be zero sum for the metropolitan region. Similarly, the Milwaukee examples cannot be justified, in terms of counteracting market failures, in that they directed new jobs to higher-unemployment cities within the metropolitan region. In the GE Healthcare and Summit Place cases, the jobs did not go to the locality (Milwaukee) with the highest unemployment rate: in April 2009, Milwaukee's unemployment rate was 11.3 percent, versus 6.3 percent for Wauwatosa (where GE Healthcare moved) and 9.5 percent for West Allis (where Summit Place is located).[16]

Similarly, there is little basis for an argument that the incentives in Milwaukee helped counteract the regressive chain of events resulting from companies' avoiding poorer cities with poor residents. Milwaukee, with a median household income of $36,187, offered incentives to Anthem to encourage it not to relocate to Summit Place in West Allis; the company turned down the incentives and relocated anyway, and the median household income in West Allis is $45,666.[17] Clearly, incentives are not enough to entice a company if the bottom line dictates otherwise. As for GE Healthcare's move, Wauwatosa's median household income, at $62,611, is 73 percent higher than Milwaukee's. In Manpower's move, certainly Milwaukee's median household income at $36,187 is much less than Glendale's $63,038. However, the problematical issue about providing expensive incentives to move the company from Glendale to Milwaukee was that only one-third of the jobs were held by City of Milwaukee residents; two-thirds were held by residents who lived outside the city, in Milwaukee County.

Of additional concern is that, through the prolific use of TIF, localities are foregoing the tax increment from the new developments until the TIF bonds are paid back. To the extent that companies are not seriously considering relocating outside the Milwaukee metropolitan area in the first place, the foregone tax increment is public revenue that could have been spent on more productive investment such as transportation infrastructure or worker training.

Corporations are nationally and internationally mobile, certainly, but perhaps more place-dependent than they admit.[18] In fact, the Milwaukee cases are not examples of globalization. GE Healthcare and Manpower consolidated their operations near their existing facilities—they likely never intended to move outside the metropolitan region, yet squeezed out incentives simply because they could. Anthem's decision to move to Summit Place without incentives was ultimately based on the bottom line; incentives only work if the new location is already optimal for a company (including being within commuting range for existing workers, given the high cost of training a new workforce at a distant location).

Yet government officials face pressure to win corporate investment. The problem is that city mayors and economic development officials are viewed as successful not only if they offer incentives and win a company, but also if they offer incentives and lose, because at least they competed. This situation contributes to the culture of competition that raises incentive offers and increases the opportunity for corporations to play one locality against another. In fact, state and local governments feel forced to compete even when they recognize the drawbacks. This quote from a 2006 letter from the Milwaukee Department of City Development's commissioner to a city council member captures this dilemma:

> We do not view this Manpower proposal as a precedent-setting endeavor—it might be viewed as "keeping up with the Joneses but this deal fairly accurately reflects the market for corporate relocations. One only need examine the GE Medical relocation to the County Research Park in Wauwatosa to see that other municipalities are utilizing any number of incentives to relocate employers. . . . That project consolidated three GE Medical operations within the region under one roof, which will facilitate

future expansion at the site. These are exactly the same parame-
ters under which Manpower will relocate from Glendale and
Brookfield to our downtown.[19]

The use of site location consultants further inflates the size of the
incentive offers. CB Richard Ellis earned its success fee—a good
investment by both GE and Manpower, and in time by Astronautics.
Moreover, the discourse surrounding a company's relocation
merely heightens the competitive element. This quote from the *Milwaukee Small Business Times* in 2006 is illustrative: "The Summit
Place office complex in West Allis has lured another tenant away
from downtown Milwaukee. The Wisconsin Dental Association
(WDA) and its thirty-five employees moved there from . . . downtown Milwaukee . . . Summit Place is snagging other office tenants
away from downtown Milwaukee."[20]

Recognizing the drawbacks of competing for investment is not
enough, as previously noted, to prevent wasteful competition. The
Milwaukee 7 was launched in 2005 as a public-private agency that
would seek to attract and retain businesses for the seven-county metropolitan region. It was funded by $12 million in public and private
support; organizers included the Metropolitan Milwaukee Association of Commerce. The M7 Code of Ethics comprises thirteen standards, including: "Members will not solicit intra-region company
relocations."[21] But this standard is wholly irrelevant if a company
uses a site location consultant; after all, a locality is not engaged in
poaching jobs from another locality if a site location consultant
approaches the locality first, as is usually the case in high-profile relocations like GE Healthcare, Manpower, and Astronautics.

Further, the extent to which significant progress must still be
made toward achieving a regional perspective is illustrated by this
quote from the *Milwaukee Journal Sentinel* in 2009: "Signs remain

that the M-7 notion of a coordinated economic effort hasn't caught on. The M-7 hosted a Waukesha County 'outreach meeting' Tuesday, but many participants left before it ended. Margaret Farrow, a former lieutenant governor who now leads the Waukesha County Action Network, a business alliance, even questioned whether the name 'Milwaukee 7' was too Milwaukee-centric."[22]

Concluding Comments

Within the context of sustaining cities and the culture of competition, it is useful to briefly consider the European context. Local governments in Europe generally have relatively limited capacity to compete for corporate investment, compared to their U.S. counterparts. In countries with centralized political systems, like Ireland, local governments have little control over their own tax base and so cannot offer tax breaks. Some countries also have national inward investment agencies, such as the Industrial Development Authority (IDA) Ireland, that prevent wasteful zero-sum competition among local governments: all major foreign corporations considering investing in Ireland must go through the IDA. In addition, the European Union (EU) Competition Policy prohibits government subsidies for companies, on the grounds that they distort competition and the efficient operation of the market (although there are equity exceptions to help promote investment in underdeveloped parts of the EU, such as, in the past, in Ireland).

On the one hand, such an interventionist framework is not transferable to the United States, where state and local government have much greater autonomy than in Europe. On the other hand, the Obama administration's urban policy is a proactive approach that seeks a balance between building economically competitive, socially equitable, and environmentally sustainable metropolitan regions around new infrastructure and other urban programs, on the one hand, and, on the other, a neoliberal urban policy that reflects a pragmatic approach grounded in the goal of metropolitan job creation through partnering with private companies (including, for example, the $200 million in planning and matching grants for businesses in regional clusters of next-generation industries).

The Obama administration's policy website explicitly reflects an integrated regional approach to urban policy, "that disregards traditional jurisdictional boundaries, setting policy that takes into account how cities, suburbs, and exurbs interact."[23] The tradition of U.S. urban economic development is firmly grounded in limited federal intervention and fiscal localism. However, this more activist White House may be able to encourage more coordinated local decision making and metropolitan partnerships, while discouraging the wasteful excesses of the dominant culture of competition. If so, state and local governments may be able to not only leverage new federal urban resources, but also increasingly to compete with, rather than against, each other for corporate investment and jobs.

NOTES

1. Rich Kirchen, "Astronautics Seeking New HQ Site," *Business Journal,* September 5, 2008. http://milwaukee.bizjournals.com/milwaukee/stories/2008/09/08/story3.html; Rob Kirchen, "Astronautics' HQ draws High Interest," *Business Journal,* February 27, 2009. http://milwaukee.bizjournals.com/milwaukee/stories/2009/03/02/story3.html.

2. Peter Fisher, "Tax Incentives and the Disappearing State Corporate Income Tax," *State Tax Notes* 23 (2002): 767–774; Greg LeRoy, "Nine Concrete Ways to Curtail the Economic War among the States," in *Reining in the Competition for Capital,* ed. Ann R. Markusen (Kalamazoo, Mich.: W. E. Upjohn Institute for Employment Research, 2007), 183–197; Markusen, ed., *Reining in the Competition for Capital;* Linda McCarthy, "The Commerce Clause as a Constraint on Business Incentives for Firms: Roadblock or a Bump in the Road in the 'Race to the Bottom?'" *Tijdschrift voor Economische en Sociale Geografie* 98 (2007): 482–492.

3. Herbert J. Rubin, "Shoot Anything That Flies; Claim Anything That Falls: Conversations with Economic Development Practitioners," *Economic Development Quarterly* 2 (1988): 236–251.

4. Kenneth P. Thomas, *Investment Incentives: Growing Use, Uncertain Benefits, Uneven Controls* (Geneva: International Institute for Sustainable Development, 2007).

5. Joel Dresang and Steve Schultze, "Millions for jobs worth it? State parcels out business aid without evidence of effectiveness." *JSOnline (Milwaukee Journal Sentinel)*, July 1, 2007. http://www.jsonline.com/news/wisconsin/29263794.html

6. Melvin L. Burstein and Arthur J. Rolnick, "Congress Should End the Economic War among the States," *The Region* 9 (1995): 3–20; Margaret E. Dewar, "Why State and Local Economic Development Programs Cause So Little Economic Development," *Economic Development Quarterly* 12 (1998): 68–87; Fisher, "Tax Incentives and the Disappearing State Corporate Income Tax": 767–774; Jane G. Gravelle, "What Can Private Investment Accomplish? The Case of the Investment Tax Credit," *National Tax Journal* 46 (1993): 275–290; William Schweke, Carl Rist, and Brian Dabson, *Bidding for Business: Are Cities and States Selling Themselves Short?* (Washington, D.C.: Corporation for Enterprise Development, 1994); Roger Wilson, *State Business Incentives and Economic Growth: Are They Effective? A Review of the Literature* (Lexington, Ky.: The Council of State Governments, 1989).

7. Timothy J. Bartik, *Who Benefits from State and Local Economic Development Policies?* (Kalamazoo, Mich.: W. E. Upjohn Institute for Employment Research, 1991); Burstein and Rolnick, "Congress Should End the Economic War among the States," 3–20.

8. John P. Blair and Robert Premus, "Major Factors in Industrial Location: A Review," *Economic Development Quarterly* 1 (1987): 72–85; Burstein and Rolnick, "Congress Should End the Economic War among the States," 3–20; John M. Levy, "The U.S. Experience with Local Economic Development," *Environment and Planning C: Government and Policy* 10 (1992): 51–60; Dennis Tosh, Troy A. Festervand, and James R. Lumpkin, "Industrial Site Selection Criteria: Are Economic Developers, Manufacturers, and Industrial Real Estate Brokers Operating on the Same Wave Length?" *Economic Development Review* 6 (1988), 62–67.

9. Herbert J. Rubin, "Symbolism and Economic Development Work: Perceptions of Urban Economic Development Practitioners," *American Review of Public Administration* 19 (1989): 233–248; Harold L. Wolman, "Local Economic Development Policy: What Explains the Divergence between Policy Analysis and Political Behavior?" *Journal of Urban Affairs* 10 (1988): 19–28.

10. John M. Levy, "The U.S. Experience with Local Economic Development": 51–60; Harold L. Wolman with David Spitzley, "The Politics of Local Economic Development," *Economic Development Quarterly* 10 (1996): 115–150.

11. Robert Guskind, "The New Civil War," *National Journal* 25 (1993): 817–821; John Hood, "Ante Freeze: Stop the State Bidding Wars for Big Business," *Policy Review* 68 (1994): 62–67.

12. Charles P. Oman, *Policy Competition for Foreign Direct Investment: A Study of Competition among Governments to Attract FDI* (Paris: OECD Development Centre, 2000).

13. Linda McCarthy, "The *Keep Jeep in Toledo Campaign:* A Lost Opportunity for the Wheels of Change?" *Tijdschrift voor Economische en Sociale Geografie* 95 (2004): 392–404.

14. Edward M. Graham and Paul R. Krugman, *Foreign Direct Investment in the United States* (Washington, D.C.: Institute for International Economics, 1991).

15. Ibid.; Charles Mahtesian, "Saving the States from Each Other: Can Congress Dictate an End to the Great Smokestack Chase?" *Governing* 10 (1996): 15; Oman, *Policy Competition for Foreign Direct Investment*.

16. Wisconsin Department of Workforce Development, *April Local Unemployment Rates Announced* (Madison, Wis.: DWD, 2009).

17. Found on www.bestplaces.net

18. Kevin R. Cox and Andrew J. Mair, "Locality and Community in the Politics of Local Economic Development," *Annals of the Association of American Geographers* 78 (1988): 307–325.

19. Letter dated February 6, 2006, from Rocky Marcoux, commissioner of Milwaukee's Department of City Development, to Michael J. Murphy, city alderman. http://legistar.milwaukee.gov/attachments/769cd5ff-8981–489f-98e4–149697316e65.PDF

20. "Summit Place Lures Another Tenant from Milwaukee," *Milwaukee Small Business Times,* February 7, 2006. http://www.biztimes.com/daily/2006/2/7/summit-place-lures-another-tenant-from-milwaukee.

21. Milwaukee 7, *Milwaukee 7 Code of Ethics,* November 29, 2006. http://www.choosemilwaukee.com/upload/documents/Milwaukee%207%20Code%20of%20Ethics.pdf.

22. John Schmid, "Ramp It Up, CEOs Tell Milwaukee 7," *JSOnline (Milwaukee Journal Sentinel),* March 4, 2007. http://www.jsonline.com/business/29250389.html.

23. See http://www.whitehouse.gov/issues/urban_policy.

REFRAMING HOUSING VALUE

Sherry Ahrentzen

Housing is fundamental to sustaining the quality of our cities: how we conceive, craft, conserve, and transform our residential communities shapes the health and vitality of our civic realm. Yet how we characterize and value housing in this country has been parochial. A narrow, privatized construct of housing value—most visible in economic positions of affordability and ownership, but also lurking in our social assessments of status, entitlement, and citizenry—has contributed to the sanitized and sometimes even crumbling nature of many American communities that cannot survive as a monoculture. Take, for example, the Phoenix area where I lived until recently, which has long been characterized by its series of monocultures: Sun City for retired seniors; Biltmore Estates for retired sports celebrities; Paradise Valley for its venture capitalists; Apache Junction for its snowbirds' mobile home parks; the ten-year-old fringe city of Maricopa for its "affordable" subdivisions financed by subprime mortgages; and so on. These monocultures survive, for the most part, by preying outside their borders. By depleting such natural resources as clean air, open space, and potable water, and requiring public investments in road, sewage, and energy lines to link a lifeline to the more diverse mothership, they transfer some of

their costs to those of the larger public realm. To maintain
needed services and activities, workers must commute from one
place to another (e.g., the landscapers and grocery store cashiers
who drive from their homes across the county to their workplaces
in Paradise Valley).

Popular phrases like *ownership society* and *cocooning* and the
growth of homeowners' associations and gated communities that
characterized residential trends of the last couple of decades dimin-
ish the extraordinarily dynamic and public face of homes embedded
in our physical and cultural landscape. Homes fortify, or cripple,
our educational systems, economic security, employment opportunities, and our individual and social health and development. Having witnessed the recent economic meltdown that was precipitated
by the highly unregulated mortgage market, most citizens today are
acutely aware how housing is the bedrock of national and global
financial markets and of powerful construction and real estate
industries.

Instead of *the ownership society* (and similar terms being promulgated today as they were in the Bush administration era), today's
city officials and citizens talk about *sustainability* and *sustainable
housing*. But again this rhetoric is too often narrowly construed: sustainable housing means more than LEED-certified buildings, solar
panels on the roof, or a deed to a home; here again, the rhetoric
often focuses on valuing the individual, privatized household or residence. But by embracing *biodiversity* as a fundamental tenet underpinning healthy residential landscapes, we can craft a sustainable
platform on which our cities can thrive. Biodiversity includes not
simply a variety of living organisms but also the diverse ecosystems
of natural habitats that effectively accommodate differing varieties
of life and the ways in which species interact with each other. In
terms of human settlements, an economically diverse city is a

resilient one.[1] In his book *The Ecology of Commerce*, Paul Hawken claims that biodiversity is the source of all wealth.[2] To accommodate and encourage such diversity, natural and built landscapes could be designed to moderate extreme environmental factors and increase cooperative ventures among often disparate partners.[3] For sustainable housing, this would translate into generating and maintaining residential ecosystems with fine-grain landscapes and systems—environmental, social, and economic—that foster symbiosis.

If we think of valuing housing in this sustainable context (that is, biodiversity of the residential ecosystem), then housing affordability migrates from a focus on the individual household or unit to one considering community affordability in all its costs and resources: financial, environmental, human, and health. The disregard of the last few decades to recognize and debate housing policies and practices from the perspective of public costs, gains, and biases makes it increasingly difficult, yet imperative, to challenge and change social and institutional systems to those that can act to enhance diverse, healthy, and thriving residential environments.

Public Nature of Private Homes

Before considering how to enhance our residential ecosystems, it is important to first demonstrate with two examples how the singular, privatized manner of construing housing's place in the public realm is an unsustainable endeavor, notably through the ways that housing affordability is conceived and the conventional homeownership of single family homes is promulgated.

Entrenched in national economic policy, as well as the basis on which a local bank decides to lend money to a homeowner, is the construct of housing affordability. Today's conventional principle, established by the U.S. Department of Housing and Urban Development

(HUD), is that a household should not spend more than 30 percent of its income on housing. An outmoded way of thinking of housing affordability, this formula is still referenced and used across a spectrum of agencies, institutions, and housing practices. Yet this construct is not a technically produced or empirically substantiated definition but a cultural construct developed by a federal agency, albeit a construct now perceived through repeated applications as an absolute. By challenging this construct, we reveal its inadequacy for addressing the context and consequences of unaffordability. The existing construct is inadequate to assess whether or not a household is shelter-poor in today's life conditions, and its exclusive use as an affordability indicator diminishes the public and social nature—and costs—of housing.

Michael E. Stone's concept of shelter poverty refutes the conventional claim that every household can reasonably afford up to a fixed percentage of income (that is, 30 percent) for housing.[4] Stone offers instead a sliding scale of affordability that takes into account differences in household composition and income. In doing so, his shelter poverty measure does not reveal a more extensive housing affordability problem in the nation's population than shown by the conventional approach. Rather, it reveals a different composition of the problem. Some very poor households, and also many large households, who pay less than 30 percent of their incomes are shelter-poor because, after paying for their housing, they do not have enough remaining income to meet their non-shelter (food, health care, transportation) needs at a minimally adequate level. Likewise, high-income households and many small households of moderate means can afford to pay more than 30 percent of their income for housing and still obtain adequate levels of food, health care, and transportation. Stone's shelter poverty approach is a more finely honed tool than the conventional 30 percent across-the-board standard for identifying which segments of society are most vulnerable and where attention is most needed.

Other efforts that challenge the conventional housing affordability index demonstrate the public costs of ill-conceived housing. The Center for Neighborhood Technology and the Institute of Transportation Studies developed the "Housing + Transportation Index" (H+T) that takes into account the two largest and interconnected sources of most household budgets. Although the share of income devoted to housing or transportation varies among metropolitan areas, the H+T combined costs are very similar, with roughly 57 percent of household incomes spent on the combined costs of housing and transportation. Where families spend more on housing, they tend to spend less on transportation, and vice versa. In their search for homes that are affordable, many working families locate far from their workplace, dramatically increasing their transportation costs and commute times. Ironically, transportation costs are not part of the mortgage financing equation. For many such families, their transportation costs end up exceeding their housing expenses. Nationally, for every dollar a working family saves on housing, it spends seventy-seven cents more on transportation.[5]

One of the most striking findings of the study is the hidden cost of cheaper but more distant housing. Taxpayers essentially subsidize subdivisions and housing built on the urban edge by public investment in new infrastructure or in tax credits and other incentives provided to developers building on the fringe. Prior to the recession that started in 2007, census data suggested that, of the twenty fastest growing counties in the United States, fifteen were located thirty miles or more from the closest central business district, where jobs and employment tend to proliferate. This is an ecosystem stretched too far, essentially bifurcated, exacerbating the stress and strain of families commuting between home and work, but also diminishing opportunities for place-based public culture. Drive time not only replaces family time but also time spent in community and public pursuits outside of work and home. And when the housing bubble burst and the economy plummeted, the now-abandoned infrastructure of many of these so-called drive-till-you-qualify subdivisions created another monoculture dotting, for example, the urban edge of Phoenix, what Andrew Ross refers to as the "latest version of the Western ghost town."[6]

The framing of homeownership in public discourse, policy, and practices also reveals an unremitting proclivity to a singular tenure status that can lead to devastating consequences for our cities. A deliberate bias toward property owners permeates American history, although in different ways over time: from property rights for suffrage, to tax policies privileging ownership and punishing tenancy.[7] Pronouncements emanating from politicians and public officials, local to national, suggest that Americans who rent instead of own are second-class citizens. In 2007 Austan Goolsbee, then a University of Chicago economics professor and later one of President Barack Obama's senior economic advisors, warned against a crackdown on subprime lending: "For be it ever so humble, . . . there really is no place like home, even if it does come with a balloon payment mortgage."[8]

The last two decades have witnessed a seismic shift in housing policy, from providing affordable rental units to providing affordable homeownership.[9] This has been partially responsible for the steady increase in homeownership rates that hit historic highs of 69 percent during President George W. Bush's administration. Proponents claim homeownership aligns with cultural values such as freedom, industriousness, and individualism. And surveys show that large majorities of renters want to own homes eventually.[10] Proponents also claim homeownership as a way to increase household wealth, with the biggest share of this wealth emanating from property value appreciation over time. Yet as multiple recessions over the last few decades demonstrate, property appreciation is not guaranteed. Research also shows that not all homeowners build wealth through home appreciation. Yet homeownership represents a badge of social approval that comes with special privileges, such as tax breaks, that indirectly cost the public: an estimated $63 billion in 2000, a figure noticeably higher than the amount of federal support provided for all assisted-housing programs. The bulk of this tax deduction subsidy goes to middle- and upper-income homeowners; many lower-income homeowners receive no such benefits.[11] Unlike the United States, other countries with high homeownership rates—for example, Canada, the United Kingdom, and Australia—do not provide tax deductions to homeowners for mortgage interest.

Even though the homeownership advocacy rhetoric emphasizes individual household fulfillment, in reality it has a very public nature. Take, for example, the Taxpayer Relief Act of 1997 that exempted most home sales from capital gains taxes. It favored real estate interests and encouraged many Americans to think of their homes more as an investment than as a place to live. The law gave people a motive to buy more real estate, while poorly regulated, lax lending practices and low interest rates provided the means to do so. Federal Reserve economists suggest that the number of homes sold after the act passed was 17 percent higher over the last decade than it would have been without the law, and the law has been blamed in part for the housing bubble.[12]

The public push toward the ownership society rebounded not only for individuals and families. It also struck those who were not foreclosed on or overextended, as witnessed by the collateral damage of empty neighborhoods, falling property values, unemployment, even public health concerns—revealing once more that home sweet home is no island but immersed in a residential ecosystem.

Domus Diversity

There have been efforts to change the paradigm of housing in this country to one that better reflects a diverse ecosystem. In recent years, the U.S. Green Building Council (USGBC) and the Congress of New Urbanism (CNU) have produced neighborhood-based planning guidelines and standards that would entail more varied land use patterns and, in theory, have a more diverse social and economic composition. The Transect Model that CNU promotes establishes a sequence of zones, moving from rural preserve to urban core within a regional planning perspective. Except for the rural zones, *residential* in these zones assumes mixed-use, higher densities, and a mix of housing types. USGBC's recent LEED-ND (neighborhood) standards target new green neighborhoods, whether infill, brownfield, or greenfield. Like much of the CNU model, LEED-ND almost exclusively focuses on land-use patterns, building types, and, to some extent, building design, with little attention to economic infrastructural changes that must coincide to foster these as sustainable communities. That is, sustainability in many of these guidelines and standards reflects energy and water and land conservation, with much less focus on social equity, human health and development, community economic investment, or civic engagement. Diversity is promulgated primarily from having different housing types, yet there is little attention to alternative residential *arrangements* (of occupancy, tenancy, activity) within those types.

These two recent neighborhood and regional planning initiatives, touting the name of sustainability, have retreated from the more inclusive and visionary planning efforts that led to the development of Columbia, Maryland, or the Greenbelt towns of the New Deal, where land use planning and building type were intertwined with social contracts: innovations in educational, recreational, religious, and healthcare services (in Columbia's case), cooperatives established for retail and commercial services, and eventually for housing (in the greenbelt towns, particularly Greenbelt, Maryland).

All of this begs the question, what do we want to sustain? For housing, is it the single-family home with a porch? Conventional mortgage lending practices? Subdivisions? From my biodiversity perspective, what needs to be sustained is a *choice* of residential options that includes but also goes beyond ensuring a diversity of housing types.[13] This includes choice of occupancy by different household living configurations,[14] of activity (for instance, many home occupations, such as taking in boarders or having a catering service, are banned in some localities), and of forms of tenancy. Our present housing market is characterized by: a singular approach to producing housing; a particular type and form of housing; and a preferred way of claiming or owning a home. Choice as a meaningful construct implies the freedom to select from a set of options, and that requires having a number of substantive, not simply stylistic, alternatives in that set from which to choose.

Similarly, planner Ruth Durack claims that "the only real quality of our present situation that is undeniably worth sustaining is our ability to make choices, or at least the availability of choices to make."[15] Referring to sustainability as "development that satisfies the choices of the present, without compromising the ability of future generations to make choices of their own," Durack suggests a *choice* platform for housing that rejects as the underlying premise fixed, preferred models of type or form, but instead argues for adopting a way of thinking about the world that accepts diversity, multiplicity, and contrast (call it *domus* diversity), and for policies and practices that encourage residential diversity in form, arrangement, and financing that can achieve such diversity without infringing on public health and safety now or in the future.

Both developing and constructing viable housing options and providing choice (beyond house models or styles) are difficult to accomplish in today's housing and regulatory markets. Take multigenerational residential arrangements, for example. There are over a dozen policies and regulations that directly or indirectly impact, even complicate or prohibit, the opportunity and availability of multigenerational living, regardless of housing form or type, including: federal financing, such as Section 202 for seniors; low-income housing tax credits (LIHTC); mortgage lending policies; Temporary Assistance to Needy Families (TANF); Social Security; Medicaid and Medicare; Fair Housing Act of 1968; and numerous local zoning, land-use, and building ordinances.

Although regulatory hurdles may seem insurmountable, some communities are beginning incremental steps to promote more housing choices in order to survive, because in these communities residential build-out, a deficit of land suitable for development, or escalating property values (and hence rising property taxes) are making it untenable to have sufficient population and economic diversity for the cities to sustain themselves. Take the accessory dwelling unit (ADU), or what is popularly called "the granny flat." ADUs are secondary (i.e., smaller) living quarters located on single-family lots, complete with separate kitchen and bathroom facilities and independent of the primary residence. ADUs can take the form of a freestanding carriage house or an apartment over a garage on the lot of a single-family house; sometimes they are appended to the main house. They are exemplars of sustainable building: no new roads to build, buildings to tear down, sewage lines to assemble. They provide small places with reasonable rent for the tenant and welcome income or support to the main-house owner. They can accommodate an older family member, or provide space for a caregiver or someone to help with the chores. Once a resident leaves, they are sometimes turned into workplaces or guest suites for visiting out-of-town relatives. The ADU is an adaptable form of housing, affordable to multiple residents, and fits into the existing texture and infrastructure of the ubiquitous subdivision neighborhood. In short, even though not promoted as "green," ADUs' affordable nature—to land, infrastructure, construction, household finances—all translate into very sustainable housing practices.

To most people, ADUs may seem innocuous, but this type of residence is illegal in many communities (the estimated number of illegal ADUs in New York City, for example, is 100,000).[16] Many communities experiencing severe affordable housing shortages find that there are a number of illegally constructed ADUs in their borders; hence communities such as Marin County, California, have passed a "Second Unit Amnesty Program." Under a state mandate in California (until recently one of the most expensive states to live in), forty-four cities and seventy counties have adopted ordinances allowing ADUs in areas zoned for single-family homes—either within the house or standing alone on the lot—in established and new neighborhoods. Santa Cruz, California, has not only changed its policies, but city officials also embraced and advocated for ADUs by making them easier to develop. In 2002, the city changed local zoning regulations to encourage the construction of ADUs; it then created a comprehensive manual for ADU planning, approval, and construction, including seven prototype designs by California architects. Further, they offered low-interest loans through a local credit union. In the first year of the new regulations, building permits for ADUs increased four-fold.[17]

Diversity and choice can also be promoted by providing more housing payment options. Currently, most residents think of their options as binary: rental/lease arrangements or conventional homeownership. Yet there is a spectrum of options between these two, some dating back decades, involving shared equity models. While they may be little known today, one in particular has gained increasing recognition and use: community land trusts (CLT).

CLTs allow one to purchase a house without the land. The CLT model has evolved in the United States over the last forty years, and today there are approximately 160 CLTs throughout thirty-eight states.[18] Conceived as a democratically controlled institution that would hold land for the common good and make it available to individuals through long-term land leases, CLT has roots in sources as diverse as: religious and ethical principles that there exist both an individual and a community interest in land; India's "Gramdan" system, in which villages act as trustees of land made available for individual use; and European and North American "land bank" programs in which public agencies hold, and then sell or lease, land, often to help preserve family farming or to encourage economic development.[19]

CLTs are nonprofit, community-based organizations with the mission to provide affordable housing in perpetuity by owning land and leasing it to those who live in houses built on that land. CLTs generally provide this lease at much lower rates than comparable for-profit or market entities. The intent of affordability in perpetuity conflicts with the propensity to use one's home as a wealth-generating mechanism, yet housing does appreciate in the CLT model, although at a lower rate than in conventionally mortgaged homes. The ground lease includes a resale formula intended to balance the interests of present homeowners with the long-term goals of the CLT and of future residents.

In most cases, CLTs have been formed as grassroots responses to specific local needs. Burlington, Vermont, has the largest community land trust in the country, with 15 percent of its homes permanently within the trust. Within the last few years, CLTs have been appearing in major cities, such as Chicago, that were witnessing a loss of younger, modest-income residents, who had little equity, as house prices escalated. The city of Irvine, California, in 2006 created a CLT with a goal of making 10 percent of the city's housing permanently low-cost (currently Irvine has a population of 180,000). Much of the low-cost housing would be newly constructed in a development on the former El Toro Marine base.[20]

"Location, location, location" is often touted as the mantra of the real estate agent. But location-efficient mortgages (LEM) interpret this maxim differently. LEMs are mechanisms that ascribe value not simply to the home but to the location of the home. LEMs increase the amount of money homebuyers are able to borrow by taking into consideration the money the buyers save by living in compact and convenient neighborhoods that require no, or minimal, use of private automobiles. Lenders establish how much a household in a particular location will likely spend on transportation by drawing on such land-use information as: population density and public transit locations, census information on car ownership, and driving levels. Accordingly, the lender calculates the difference in transportation costs between an urban household and its suburban counterpart. Taking into account savings on vehicle purchases, maintenance, insurance and fuel, this dollar amount is added onto the buyer's qualifying income. Provided by Fannie Mae until 2011, LEMs were available in Seattle, Chicago, Los Angeles, and San Francisco.

Outside the United States, where homes have not been as strongly privatized, the result is more diverse and denser residential landscapes. For example, in older segments of Amsterdam, social diversity does not depend upon or correspond with architectural or housing-type diversity, because of the substantial subsidies the state provides to reduce rents and to support households in homes more expensive than the residents could otherwise afford. Affordability is

considered in light of the community as a whole, not simply individual households. Potential hostility is reduced among social
groups living in proximate quarters, because the Dutch welfare system reduces extremes of economic difference.[21]

Another European example comes from Great Britain, where the
concept of flexible tenure has been introduced. In such arrangements, residents can move between tenure types (social, market
rent, shared ownership, full ownership) of the same property or
residence over time. Do It Yourself Shared Ownership (DIYSO),
available in England and Scotland, allows residents incremental
movement from shared ownership of their home into full ownership. Another arrangement, a form of mortgage rescue scheme
operating primarily at the national level, allows homeowners to
move from full ownership to part ownership or rental when the
need arises (for instance, a sudden income loss owing to lengthy
unemployment, illness, etc.), with the option to move back to full
ownership over time. These models are not widespread, and the
population's knowledge of, and access to, them is limited. Yet these
nascent schemes provide flexibility (of financing and tenure) and
stability (of property and residence) simultaneously, indicating an
enriched residential ecosystem.

Another exemplar that provides flexibility and stability simultaneously is cohousing development in Sweden. Swedish cohousing is
generally on a much larger scale than that in the United States. The
largest cohousing development in the country, Stoplyckan in Lin-
choping, has four hundred residents living in 184 dwelling units
spread across thirteen buildings. Also different from American
counterparts, cohousers in Stoplyckan share some of the common
rooms with public healthcare companies. These companies rent the
cohousing common spaces of the community (e.g., the dining room
or the gym) during standard business hours, after which the room

is then used by the cohousers. This commingling of spaces reduces the high cost of maintaining large common spaces during the day when few residents use them, and ensures that these spaces are used by organizations and individuals who provide a service to the community at large as well to certain segments of cohousers (e.g., seniors) who use those (generally healthcare) facilities during the day as well.

Concluding Remarks

The purpose here is to reframe housing value within a framework of sustainability by considering costs and affordability, not simply at the level of the private household, but also at the community and public scale. As a linchpin within the residential ecosystem, choice ensues through a greater diversity of residential options in terms of physical form, residential arrangement, and cultural practices of valuing (one form of this being financing). The most prominent and growing segments of our population that will dictate housing demand in the next few years—the graying (baby boomers retiring), grasping (young people enduring delayed economic productivity due to effects of recession), and variegating (immigrants settling) of our housing market—will be living with considerably fewer resources than in years past. In reframing our housing discourse and cultural values, we move the advancement of affordable housing from the concerns and circumstances of privatized households to those of the larger community and public infrastructure.

Sustainable housing—and cities—will require more than new market-based downtown lofts or mixed-income public housing conversions. Although Jane Jacobs's call for mixed use and diversity in cities infuses the perspective proposed here, she implied that markets will produce diversity of their own accord. Yet, as Susan Fainstein points out, Jacobs's critique was of a time and place that did not anticipate the impact of present market tendencies.[22] Organic development responding to and reflecting local forces and conditions cannot compete today with the interconnected web of global exchange that reaches into the smallest enclaves. Urban centers and neighborhoods were once characterized by multiple ownership and small lot sizes. Today's development is shaped by single/conglomerate ownership, vast developments focused on scalability, global financing and banking practices, imitation and duplication, and the mass production basis entrenched in our construction industry. These features, along with standardized marketing tools, have not simply restrained diversity in residential development. Rather, as Ross points out in his analysis of Phoenix, such practices have intentionally subverted that diversity, whether by the dominant pre-recession land development practices that were sanctioned by public and elected officials (the latter often with real estate development interests and holdings) or by the technical-oriented, ARRA-funded fixes of the current Green City program that neglect environmental justice and social equity.[23]

Although it is often hard to find the silver lining in this recession, one upbeat note is that it has retarded the unabated, and eventually unsustainable, residential development trajectory we were on. With the stall in rampant residential development, this may be the time to start seeding these innovations and reframing our cultural concept of housing value—and as a result, to cultivate an enriched foundation for regenerating a healthier and sustainable civic realm.

NOTES

1. President's Council on Sustainable Development, *Sustainable America: A New Consensus for Prosperity, Opportunity, and a Healthy Environment* (Washington, D.C.: President's Council, 1996).

2. Paul Hawken, *The Ecology of Commerce* (New York: HarperCollins, 1994).

3. Randolph T Hester, *Design for Ecological Democracy* (Cambridge, Mass.: MIT Press, 2006).

4. Michael E Stone, "Housing Affordability: One-Third of a Nation Shelter-Poor," in *A Right to Housing: Foundation for a New Social Agenda,* ed. Rachel G. Bratt, Michael E. Stone, and Chester Hartman (Philadelphia: Temple University Press, 2006), 38–60.

5. Barbara J. Lipman, *A Heavy Load: The Combined Housing and Transportation Burdens of Working Families* (Washington, D.C.: Center for Housing Policy, 2006).

6. Andrew Ross, *Bird on Fire: Lessons from the World's Least Sustainable City* (New York: Oxford University Press, 2011) 36

7. Donald A. Krueckeberg, "The Grapes of Rent: A History of Renting in a Country of Owners," *Housing Policy Debate* 10 (1999): 9–30.

8. Quoted in: Paul Krugman, "Home Not-So-Sweet Home," *New York Times,* June 23, 2008, A25.

9. William M. Rohe and Harry L. Watson, eds., *Chasing the American Dream: New Perspectives on Affordable Homeownership* (Ithaca, N.Y.: Cornell University Press, 2007).

10. Fannie Mae Foundation, *Fannie Mae National Housing Survey* (Washington, D.C.: Fannie Mae Foundation, 2002).

11. Rohe and Watson, *Chasing the American Dream.*

12. Vikas Bajaj and David Leonhardt, "Tax Break May Have Helped Cause Housing Bubble," *New York Times,* December 19, 2008. http://www.nytimes.com/2008/12/19/business/19tax.html.

13. Sherry Ahrentzen, "Choice in Housing," *Harvard Design Magazine* (Summer 1999): 62–67.

14. Sherry Ahrentzen, "Family Embeddedness," in *Unintended Consequences,* ed. Julie Ross (Tempe, Ariz.: Arizona Board of Regents for and on behalf of College of Design, Arizona State University, 2007).

15. Ruth Durack, "Village Vices: The Contradiction of New Urbanism and Sustainability," *Places* 14 (2001): 64–69.

16. Chhaya Community Development Corporation, *Illegal Dwelling Units: A Potential Source of Affordable Housing in New York City* (New York: Chhaya Community Development Corporation, 2008).

17. Martin C. Pedersen, "The Granny Flat Grows Up," *Metropolis* (November 2005): 32.

18. Rosalind Greenstein and Yesim Sungu-Eryilmaz, "Community Land Trusts: Leasing Land for Affordable Housing," *Land Lines Newsletter* 17 (April 2005): 8–10.

19. Tom Peterson, "Community Land Trusts: An Introduction," *Planners Web.com: Planning Commissioners Journal* 23 (Summer 1996). http://www.plannersweb.com/wfiles/w162.html.

20. Stephen Clark, "Irvine Locking in Low-Cost Housing," *Los Angeles Times,* April 1, 2006. http://articles.latimes.com/2006/apr/01/local/me-landtrust1.

21. Susan S. Fainstein, "Cities and Diversity: Should We Want It? Can We Plan For It?" *Urban Affairs Quarterly* 41 (2005): 3–19.

22. Ibid.

23. Ross, *Bird.*

PART II

URBAN PRACTICES

CONNECTING COMMUNITIES

NOTES TOWARD A HISTORY
OF AGRARIAN URBANISM

Charles Waldheim

The agrarian and the urban are two categories of thought that have more often than not been opposed to one another. Across many disciplines, and for many centuries, the city and the country have been called upon to define each other through a binary opposition. Contemporary design culture and discourse on cities are, by contrast, awash in claims of the potential for urban agriculture. Enthusiasm for agricultural production in and around cities has grown through an increased environmental literacy on behalf of designers and scholars. Equally, this renewed interest in the relation of food production to urban form has been made possible by increased public literacy about food and the forms of industrial food production and distribution that characterize globalization. This renewed interest in food production and consumption has been shaped by a variety of authors and interests, but has been most forcefully felt as a call for more renewable or sustainable agricultural practices associated with local food production, reduced carbon footprint, increased public health, and the associated benefits of preindustrial farming techniques including increased biodiversity and ecological health. These tendencies have been most clearly articulated through the so-called slow food and locavore movements. Although much has been written on the implications of these tendencies for agricultural production, public policy, and food as an element of culture, little has been written on the potentially profound implications of these transformations for the shape and structure of the city itself. Much of the enthusiasm for slow and local food in the context of urban populations has been predicated on the assumption that abandoned or underused brownfield sites could be remediated and repurposed with productive potential. Equally, this enthusiasm for urban agriculture has been based on the rededication of greenfield sites peripheral to the city, focusing valuable ecological assets on food production rather than on suburban sprawl. Although both of these remain viable and laudable goals, they shed little light on the implications of such transformations on the shape and the structure of urban form. For those interested in the city as an object of study and subject of design, further inquiry into the possibilities for an agricultural urbanism is needed. The present essay proposes a history of urban form conceived through the spatial, ecological, and infrastructural implications of agricultural production. In the projects that form this tentative counter-history, agricultural production is conceived as a formative element of the city's structure, rather than considered as adjunct to, outside of, or inserted within traditional urban forms. Although such a counter-history may remain alternative or even marginal, it may be found useful as architects and urbanists grapple with the implications for urban form attendant to their renewed interest in the agricultural. This alternative history of the city seeks to construct a useful past from three urban projects organized explicitly around agricultural production as inherent to the economic, ecological, and spatial order of the city.

Many projects of twentieth-century urban planning explicitly aspired to construct an agrarian urbanism. Often these agrarian aspirations were an attempt to reconcile the seemingly contradictory impulses of the industrial metropolis with the social and cultural conditions of agrarian settlement. In many of these projects, agrarianism came to stand as an alternative to the dense metropolitan form of industrial arrangement that grew from the great migrations from farm village to industrial city in the nineteenth- and early twentieth-century cities of Western Europe and North America. The agrarian aspirations of many modernist urban planning proposals lie, in the first instance, in the relatively decentralized model of industrial order favored by Henry Ford and other industrialists as early as the 1910s and 1920s. Following Ford's organizational preference for spatial decentralization, industrial organizations tended to spread horizontally and to abandon the traditional industrial city. In part as a response to the social conditions of the Depression, agrarianism came to be seen as a form of continuity between formerly agrarian populations based on subsistence farming and the relatively vulnerable industrial workforce of the modern metropolis. By mixing industry with agriculture, many modernist urban planners imagined, there could be a rotational labor system in which workers alternated between factory jobs and collective farms. Most often, these new spatial orders were understood as vast regional landscapes, and their representation conflated aerial view and map.

The emergence of these tendencies in the twentieth century might be read through three unbuilt projects advocating a decentralized agrarian urbanism: Frank Lloyd Wright's "Broadacre City" (1934–1935), Ludwig Hilberseimer's "New Regional Pattern" (1945–1949), and Andrea Branzi's "Agronica" (1993–1994) or "Territory for the New Economy" (1999).[1] Even though these projects were produced decades apart by three very different authors, taken collectively they illustrate the implications for urban form of agricultural production as inherent to the structure of the city. These projects also form a coherent genealogy of thought on the subject of agricultural urbanism, as Branzi explicitly references Hilberseimer's urban proposals, and Hilberseimer's work was informed by familiarity with Wright's urban project. Each of the projects presented their audiences with a profound reconceptualization of the city, proposing radical decentralization and dissolution of the urban figure into a productive landscape. This dissolution of figure into field had the effect of rendering the classical distinction between city and countryside irrelevant, in favor of a conflated condition of suburbanized regionalism. From the perspective of contemporary interests in urban agriculture, all three projects offer equally compelling alternatives to the canonical history of urban form.

Implicit in the work of these three urbanists was the assumption of an ongoing process of urban decentralization led by industrial economy. For Wright, Hilberseimer, and Branzi, the decreased density that urbanism produced through the new industrial logic of decentralization came to depend upon landscape as the primary medium of urban form. These suburban landscapes were embodied and fleshed out with agricultural lands, farms, and fields. These projects proposed large territorial or regional networks of urban infrastructure bringing existing natural environments into relationship with new agricultural and industrial landscapes.

BROADACRES/USONIA

In the depths of the Depression, lacking reasonable prospects for a recovery of his once towering stature as the dean of American architects, Frank Lloyd Wright persuaded his lone remaining patron to fund a traveling exhibition of Wright's conception of an organic American urbanism. Broadacre City, as it was referred to, consisted of a large model and supporting materials produced by student apprentices at Taliesin in the winter of 1934–1935. Although the premises underpinning the project were evident in Wright's lectures as early as the 1920s and fully informed Wright's 1932 publication *The Disappearing City*, the Broadacre model and drawings debuted in a 1935 New York City exhibition. Subsequently, the traveling exhibition toured extensively, and the remarkably durable project was subsequently disseminated in publications including *When Democracy Builds* (1945) and *The Living City* (1958).[2]

Broadacre City offered American audiences the clearest crystallization of Wright's damning critique of the modern industrial city, positing Broadacre as an autochthonous organic model for North American settlement across an essentially boundless carpet of cultivated landscape. Eschewing traditional European distinctions between city and countryside, Broadacre proposed a network of transportation and communication infrastructures using the Jeffersonian grid as its principal ordering system. Within this nearly undifferentiated field, the county government (headed by the county architect) replaced other levels of government, administering a population of landowning citizen-farmers. Wright was clearly conversant with and sympathetic to Henry Ford's notion of a decentralized settlement pattern for North America, and the closest built parallel for Wright's work on Broadacre can be found in Ford's instigation of what would become the Tennessee Valley Authority (TVA). The TVA was charged with the construction of hydroelectric dams and highways along the Tennessee River, in the electrification of an entire region as a seeding process for future urbanization.[3]

Enjoying ownership of one acre of land per person as a birthright, residents of Broadacre (or Usonia, as Wright would come to refer to it) were to enjoy modern houses set amid ample subsistence gardens and small-scale farms. This basic pattern of variously scaled housing and landscape types was interspersed with light industry, small commercial centers and markets, civic buildings, and of course the ubiquitous highway. In spite of the project's extremely low density, most of the ground was cleared and cultivated. Occasionally, this constructed and maintained landscape relented in favor of extant waterways, topographic features, or other preexisting ecologies. Presumably the extrapolation of Broadacre City from its chiefly midwestern origins to the margins of the continent would have been accomplished with varying degrees of accommodation to local climate, geography, and geology, if not cultural or material history. The status of previously urbanized areas existing outside of Wright's Broadacre remained open; presumably these would be abandoned in place, again following Ford's lead.

Wright's critique of private ownership, conspicuous consumption, and the accumulation of wealth associated with cities was no small part of the explicit social critique offered by Broadacre, as the worst of the Depression forced bankrupt family farmers to flee their mortgaged farms in the Midwest for protest in the East or California in the West. Ironically, given his anxiety over the corrosive effects of accumulated wealth and speculative capital, Wright found in Ford's notion of regional infrastructure the basis for an American pattern of organic urban development. Wright's Broadacre provided a respite from the relentless demands of profit associated with the industrial city, even as the American city was well on a course toward decentralization, a course itself driven by the decentralizing tendencies of Fordist production.

THE NEW REGIONAL PATTERN/THE NEW CITY

Another modernist architect/urbanist grappling with the impacts of decentralization on urban form was Ludwig Hilberseimer. Born and educated in Karlsruhe, Germany, Hilberseimer worked with Mies van der Rohe at the Bauhaus until the rise of fascism precipitated their emigration to Chicago and the Armour Institute of Technology (later, IIT) in 1938. Hilberseimer is most notorious for his earlier studies for totalizing rationally planned schemes of modern urbanism from the 1920s such as *Hochhausstadt* (Highrise City, 1924), but he quickly abandoned those schemes in favor of projects that explored decentralization and landscape as remedies to the ills of the industrial city. This was evident as early as a 1927 sketch titled "The Metropolis as a Garden-City."[4] Hilberseimer's work over the course of the 1930s was clearly influenced by European precedents for the garden city and evidenced a strategy for the use of landscape and mixed-height housing in a low-density pattern. This is a pattern that would continue to appear in his work in the United States over the following decades. Particularly formative in this regard was Hilberseimer's project for mixed-height housing in the 1930s, the principles of which would inform the balance of his career. Hilberseimer during this period was committed to the inevitable decentralization of the traditional city as the resultant of industrial policy. This tendency was evident to him as early as the 1920s, in Henry Ford's decision during the previous decade to relocate industrial production outside the city of Detroit.

By the 1940s, Hilberseimer's notion of the settlement unit took clearer form, anticipating the development of an interstate highway system, articulating precise relationships between transportation networks, settlement units, and the regional landscape. Hilberseimer's interest in an organic urbanism for the North American continent was further fueled by civil defense imperatives toward decentralization, in the years following World War II.[5] In the wake of Hiroshima, Hilberseimer adapted his proposals to anticipate the construction of the interstate highway system as a civil defense infrastructure and an extension of Fordist production logics. In this context, and conversant with Wright's Broadacre

City as well as the progressive TVA project and its proponents in
the Regional Planning Association of America, Hilberseimer
developed his new regional pattern as a strategy for the urbanization of a low-density North American settlement pattern based on
regional highway systems and natural environmental conditions.
Hilberseimer disseminated his proposals through a publication,
*The New Regional Pattern: Industries and Gardens, Workshops and
Farms* (1949). The principles and analysis informing his project
were published prior to the project itself, in *The New City: Principles of Planning* (1944), and disseminated a decade later in *The
Nature of Cities* (1955).[6]

Like Broadacre, the New Regional Pattern was organized around
the distribution of transportation and communication networks
across an essentially horizontal landscape. Within this extensive
horizontal territory, housing, farms, light industry, commercial
buildings, and civic spaces formed variously scaled networks across
a field of decentralized distribution. The New Regional Pattern's
organizational structure did not defer to the abstraction of the grid,
but rather was informed by the natural environment: topography,
hydrology, vegetation, wind patterns, and the like. It conflated
infrastructural systems with built landscapes and found environmental conditions to produce a radically reconceived settlement
pattern for the North American continent. Although Hilberseimer's
exquisite drawings (many not his but the uncredited work of IIT
colleague Alfred Caldwell) did not make an explicit case for the kind
of ecological awareness apparent in contemporary landscape urbanism, they clearly inflected urban infrastructure to ambient environmental conditions.[7] In this regard, the project offers a profound
critique of traditional urban form, and of the inadequacy of traditional city planning discourse to deal with the social and technological conditions of the modern age.

Agronica/Territory for the New Economy

The work of the Italian architect and urbanist Andrea Branzi is equally relevant to the emergent discourse on agrarian urbanism. Branzi's work reanimates a long tradition of using urban project as social and cultural critique. This form of urban projection deploys a project not simply as an illustration or "vision," but rather as a demystified distillation and description of present urban predicaments. In this sense, one might read Branzi's urban projects not as a possible utopia, but rather as a critically engaged and politically literate delineation of the power structures, forces, and flows shaping the contemporary urban condition. Over the course of the past four decades, Branzi's work has articulated a remarkably consistent critique of the social, cultural, and intellectual poverty of much laissez-faire urban development and of the realpolitik assumptions of much urban design and planning. As an alternative, Branzi's projects propose urbanism in the form of an environmental, economic, and aesthetic critique of the failings of the contemporary city.

Born and educated in Florence, Branzi studied architecture in a cultural milieu of the Operaists, and a scholarly tradition of Marxist critique as evidenced through use of speculative urban proposals for cultural criticism. Branzi first came to international visibility as a member of the collective Archizoom (mid-1960s), based in Milan but associated with the Florentine Architettura Radicale movement. Archizoom's project and texts for No-Stop City (1968–1971) illustrate an urbanism of continuous mobility, fluidity, and flux. Although No-Stop City was received on one level as a satire of the British technophilia of Archigram, it was received on another level as an illustration of an urbanism without qualities, a representation of the degree-zero conditions for urbanization.[8]

Archizoom's use of typewriter keystrokes on A4 paper to represent a nonfigural planning study for No-Stop City anticipated contemporary interest in indexical and parametric representations of the city. The group's work prefigured current interest in describing the relentlessly horizontal field conditions of the modern metropolis as a surface shaped by the strong forces of economic and ecological flows. Equally, these drawings and their texts anticipate current interest in infrastructure and ecology as nonfigurative drivers of urban form. A generation of contemporary urbanists has drawn from Branzi's intellectual commitments. The diverse list of influenced interests ranges from Stan Allen and James Corner's interest in field conditions to Alex Wall and Alejandro Zaera Polo's interest in logistics.[9] More recently, Pier Vittorio Aureli and Martino Tattara's project Stop-City directly references Branzi's use of nonfigurative urban projection as a form of social and political critique.[10] Equally, Branzi's urban projects are available to inform contemporary interests within architectural culture and urbanism on topics as diverse as animalia, indeterminacy, genericity, and others.

As a deliberately nonfigurative urbanism, No-Stop City renewed and disrupted a longstanding tradition of nonfigurative urban projection as socialist critique. In this regard, Branzi's No-Stop City draws upon the urban planning projects and theories of Ludwig Hilberseimer, particularly Hilberseimer's New Regional Pattern and that project's illustration of a proto-ecological urbanism.[11]

Not coincidentally, both Branzi and Hilberseimer chose to illustrate the city as a continuous system of relational forces and flows, as opposed to a collection of objects. In this regard, the ongoing recuperation of Hilberseimer, and Branzi's renewed relevance for discussions of contemporary urbanism, render them particularly relevant to discussions of ecological urbanism. Andrea Branzi occupies a singular historical position as a hinge figure between the social and environmental aspirations of modernist planning of the postwar era, and the politics of 1968 in which his work first emerged for

English-language audiences. Thus his work is particularly well suited to shed light on the emergent discussion around ecological urbanism.

Branzi's Agronica project (1993–1994) illustrates the relentlessly horizontal spread of capital across thin tissues of territory, and the resultant "weak urbanization" that the neoliberal economic paradigm affords. Agronica embodies the potential parallelism between agricultural and energy production, new modalities of post-Fordist industrial economy, and the cultures of consumption that these construct.[12] More recently, in 1999, Branzi (with the Domus Academy, a postgraduate research institute founded in the 1980s) executed a project for Philips in Eindhoven. These projects returned to the recurring themes in Branzi's oeuvre, with typical wit and pith, illustrating a Territory for the New Economy in which agricultural production was a prime factor in deriving urban form.[13]

Branzi's "weak work" maintains its critical and projective relevance for a new generation of urbanists interested in the economic and agricultural drivers of urban form. His longstanding call for the development of weak urban forms and nonfigural fields has already influenced the thinking of those who articulated landscape urbanism over a decade ago, and promises to reanimate emergent discussions of ecological urbanism.[14] Equally, Branzi's projective and polemic urban propositions promise to shed light on the proposition of agrarian urbanism, and on its potential for shaping the contemporary city and the disciplines describing it.

Although this brief prehistory of agricultural urbanism raises more questions than it answers, it seems a useful (if not necessary) exercise in understanding the broader implications of contemporary food culture for the design disciplines. In this regard, it is significant that each of the three architects/urbanists presented here as pursuing an explicitly agricultural urbanism did so as part of a broader critical position engaged with economic inequality, social justice, and environmental health. Wright, Hilberseimer, and Branzi, each in his own way, embodied a longstanding tradition of using urban proposals as a form of social critique in which the production and consumption of the city, its economy and ecology, are available as tools of analysis and critique. Although Wright, Hilberseimer, and Branzi were each responding to different economic and ecological contexts, each in his way found the urban project an effective vehicle for critiquing the form of their contemporary cities and the economic, social, and political orders producing them.

NOTES

1. Frank Lloyd Wright, *The Living City* (New York: Horizon Press, 1958); Ludwig Hilberseimer, *The New Regional Pattern: Industries and Gardens, Workshops and Farms* (Chicago: Paul Theobald and Co., 1949); Andrea Branzi, D. Donegani, A. Petrillo, and C. Raimondo, "Symbiotic Metropolis: Agronica," in *The Solid Side,* ed. Ezio Manzini and Marco Susani (Netherlands: V+K Publishing / Philips, 1995), 101–120; and Andrea Branzi, "Preliminary Notes for a Master Plan," and "Master Plan Strijp Philips, Eindhoven 1999," *Lotus* 107 (2000): 110–123.

2. The principles underpinning Wright's Broadacre project were published in 1932, in Frank Lloyd Wright, *Disappearing City* (New York: W. F. Payson, 1932), and subsequently reformulated as *When Democracy Builds* (Chicago: University of Chicago Press, 1945). For an historical overview of Broadacre's influence and contemporary reception, see Peter Hall, *Cities of Tomorrow* (Oxford: Blackwell, 1996), 285–290.

3. For an overview of the Tennessee Valley Authority, see Walter Creese, *TVA's Public Planning* (Knoxville: University of Tennessee Press, 1990), and Hall, *Cities,* 161–163.

4. For an overview of the origins of Hilberseimer's interpretation of the garden city, see David Spaeth, "Ludwig Hilberseimer's Settlement Unit: Origins and Applications," in *In the Shadow of Mies: Ludwig Hilberseimer, Architect, Educator, and Urban Planner,* ed. Richard Pommer, David Spaeth, and Kevin Harrington (New York/Chicago: Rizzoli/Art Institute of Chicago, 1988), 54–68.

5. Hilberseimer and Caldwell advocated for decentralization as a civil defense strategy in the wake of Hiroshima. See Caldwell, "Atomic Bombs and

City Planning," *Journal of the American Institute of Architects* 4 (1945): 289–299, and also Hilberseimer, "Cities and Defense," (manuscript, c. 1945) reprinted in *In the Shadow of Mies,* ed. Pommer, Spaeth, and Harrington, 89–93.

6. Ludwig Hilberseimer, *The New City: Principles of Planning* (Chicago: Paul Theobald and Co., 1944); *The Nature of Cities: Origin, Growth, and Decline, Pattern and Form, Planning Problems* (Chicago: Paul Theobald and Co., 1955).

7. For a detailed account of Hilberseimer's professional relationship with Caldwell, see Caroline Constant, "Hilberseimer and Caldwell: Merging Ideologies in the Lafayette Park Landscape," in *CASE: Lafayette Park Detroit,* ed. Charles Waldheim (Cambridge/Munich: Harvard/Prestel, 2004), 95–111. On Caldwell's life and work, see Dennis Domer, *Alfred Caldwell: The Life and Work of a Prairie School Landscape Architect* (Baltimore, Md.: Johns Hopkins University Press, 1997).

8. Archizoom Associates, "No-Stop City. Residential Parkings. Climatic Universal Sistem," *Domus* 496 (March 1971): 49–55. For Branzi's reflections on the project, see Andrea Branzi, "Notes on No-Stop City: Archizoom Associates 1969–1972," in *Exit Utopia: Architectural Provocations 1956–1976,* ed. Martin van Schaik and Otakar Macel (Munich: Prestel, 2005), 177–182. For more recent scholarship on the project and its relations to contemporary architectural culture and urban theory, see Kazys Varnelis, "Programming after Program: Archizoom's No-Stop City," *Praxis* (May 2006): 82–91.

9. On field conditions and contemporary urbanism, see James Corner, "The Agency of Mapping: Speculation, Critique and Invention," in *Mappings,* ed. Denis Cosgrove (London: Reaktion Books, 1999), 213–300, and Stan Allen, "Mat Urbanism: The Thick 2-D," in *CASE: Le Corbusier's Venice Hospital and the Mat Building Revival,* ed. Hashim Sarkis (Munich: Prestel, 2001), 118–126. On logistics and contemporary urbanism, see Susan Nigra Snyder and Alex Wall, "Emerging Landscape of Movement and Logistics," *Architectural Design Profile* (1998): 16–21; and Alejandro Zaera Polo, "Order Out of Chaos: The Material Organization of Advanced Capitalism," *Architectural Design Profile* (1994): 24–29.

10. See Pier Vittorio Aureli and Martino Tattara, "Architecture as Framework: The Project of the City and the Crisis of Neoliberalism," *New Geographies* (September 2008): 38–51.

11. Hilberseimer, *The New Regional Pattern.*

12. Branzi et al., "Symbiotic Metropolis: Agronica," *Solid Side,* 101–120.

13. Branzi, "Preliminary Notes" and "Master Plan," *Lotus* 107: 110–123.

14. Andrea Branzi, "The Weak Metropolis," Paper presented to the Ecological Urbanism Conference, Harvard Graduate School of Design, April 4, 2009.

THE ART OF
PLACE-MAKING

Georgia Butina Watson

Many people today, throughout the world, seem to feel that any place, be it city or neighborhood, should have its own distinctive character, its own place identity. In an ever globalizing world, once regionally inflected built form—the kind of environment that signaled the uniqueness of a place—is no longer a given. Now, urban designers, planners, architects, landscape architects, politicians, and people from all walks of life are investigating how to achieve distinctive and positive place identities. Such places, it is argued here, are rooted in the past but are also evolving and changing to meet different cultural and societal needs. The process through which such places are shaped is called the art of place-making.

This essay first addresses the issues of local distinctiveness and place identity, and how we can achieve these through planning and design processes. A number of theories that underpin the conceptualizations of local distinctiveness, as well as place identity and its relation to our sense of personal and group identity, are discussed. The essay next proposes a conceptual framework for analyzing places from the identity perspective, and illustrates, through a case study of Angell Town, Brixton (London), how we can work collaboratively to pursue the art of place-making that creates a sense of place identity for resident users.

Searching for Identity and Place

In the past, places used to be shaped by local people employing the vernacular processes, using locally sourced materials through which most buildings and settlements were produced. Limited knowledge of structural principles and constructional techniques influenced the range of building types in any particular place, producing localized, unique solutions.[1] By the middle of the nineteenth century, in the industrializing parts of the world, these localized building traditions began to change. This was due to the mass production of building materials and relatively cheap transportation by canal and rail systems, enabling building materials to be drawn from distant sources. Scientific and technological developments also increased the range of ways in which built form was produced. New design ideas began to be spread through design books and magazines, and by a growing number of designers working across ever wider geographical areas. Now, after more than a century of these changes, regionally distinctive built form no longer happens by default. According to Michael Hough, "the question of regional character has become a question of choice and, therefore, of design rather than of necessity."[2] Building type choices offered to everyday users today, particularly in new housing, are increasingly becoming standardized, and similar typologies are being produced internationally, as a result of the globalized systems of built form production. Many critics see these built form solutions as anonymous, *anywhere* places, where space and time are converging into homogenized cultural landscapes. In contrast to such anywhere places, shaped by globalized form-production processes, cities such as Oxford, England, display a unique character and a strong sense of place identity. This is due to gradual transformation processes over time, where the city's original morphology, street pattern, and building typology all form strong associations of deep-rooted historic heritage where each new addition respected what was there before. Such cities are loved and admired by their users, and the processes through which we build such places are intrinsic to the art of place-making.

Promoting one particular understanding of what local distinctiveness and place identity might mean, for example, many professionals and organizations, such as the Commission for Architecture and the Built Environment (CABE) and design review panels, are searching for tools and methods that would enable designers and city builders to produce places that have a special character and a distinctive place identity. The shared nature of such desires provides a platform for political debates and campaigns. and the issues of place identity now engage even mainstream politicians. in many parts of the world. Local distinctiveness and place identity have also recently acquired economic salience. Place identity has become a sought-after sales commodity worldwide, "the unique selling proposition" through which localities are marketed as tourist destinations in what has become the world's largest industry.[3]

Faced with these increasingly powerful social, political, and economic pressures, many planners and designers now wish to address the issues of place identity in their work. In Great Britain, for example, the importance of place identity is embedded in national policy guidance, and such issues have begun to be addressed by designers across a wide range of professions. This concern is not merely an aspect of the British culture; it has a far wider geographical spread. In Malaysia, for example, contemporary Malaysian architects such as Jimmy Lim produce designs that are rooted in the Malaysian traditional building forms, while developing new types of urbanism capable of dealing both with the sustainability agenda and the multiculturalism specific to Malaysia and its place-identity issues.[4]

The concept of place identity enables planning and design issues to be also debated in social terms, in ways that people seem to recognize as relevant to their own everyday lives. When we get beneath the surface of what users say when they talk about a place's identity, they usually have in mind some meaning the place has in terms of their *own* identity: how the place affects the way they conceive of themselves, or how they imagine it will affect the way other people will conceive of them. The interweaving of place identity and human identity is clearly a broadly encountered phenomenon, which perhaps helps to explain why the term "identity" is used, in everyday speech, equally in relation both to places and to people.

Before we can develop any useful ideas about "how to do it," we have to develop some practice-orientated ideas about "how to think about it."[5] Until recently, most of the theoretical underpinning for understanding the concept of place identity had relied heavily on visual and aesthetic criteria. Such reliance, in the absence of other considerations, often leads to pastiche, a kind of Disneyfication where only surface design matters. However, as the sociologist Scott Lash explains, cities signify to their users complex experiences that go beyond mere visual representation.[6] As we move through a city's streets and spaces, we experience them with all our senses; they form a total environment. We inhabit such spaces. This process of inhabiting involves the whole body with all its senses, and generates meanings arising from patterns of human use as well as from the sensory associations of places themselves.

Similar ideas are put forward by David Novitz, who writes about the experience of places as a collaborative engagement, a participatory art, where users actively interpret the city through appreciative practices.[7] In this collaborative engagement we are not merely passive users: we respond to such places emotionally, through the senses, and contribute to the overall experience of such places through movement and engagement with our surroundings.

Many city places are used for carnivals, festivals, and street performances, where the buildings and open spaces provide a stage for creative collaborative art performances at which music, dance, and other types of public art engagements are celebrated. The multisensory process of inhabiting places, those landscapes shaped and modified by human intervention, geographers call creating "cultural landscapes." If we want to understand why particular types of cultural landscapes and place identities matter to so many people, we have to understand the links between the meanings people attach to cultural landscapes and the ways in which they interpret their own identities. This leads to the definition of place identity: *the set of meanings associated with any particular cultural landscape that any particular person or group of people draws on in the construction of their own personal or social identities.*[8]

As we live today in places that consist of many cultural groups, it is important to establish design principles that could strengthen a sense of place of particular settlements, yet would at the same time be seen by many different cultural groups as their own. The places that most strongly support the notion of identity, are frequently called *responsive.*[9] Such places offer a wide range of choices to different cultural groups through different spatial and built form patterns that support different types of activity and cultural interpretations. Since cultural landscapes last for a very long time, it is important that planners and designers create places that can support a great variety of functions and experiences over time. These cultural landscapes should also support many communities and should therefore be able to support many different types of individual and collective identities.

Responsiveness can be achieved through many qualities that can be seen at varying morphological levels: from such large-scale natural systems as topography, geomorphology, flora, and fauna, to such spatial structures as streets, blocks, individual plots, buildings, and their components. How people respond to these environments, and to other people within them, is key. It is very important that we design places that are accessible, connected, and permeable, where we can encounter other users and so explore such places without fear. Popular, people-oriented places generate many associated activities, contributing to the vitality of the areas we inhabit. The safer the places, the more they are used; the more they are used the more vitality they generate. Such places generate functions that contribute to the users' sense of place and place identity.

Another important aspect of responsiveness is the ability of users to find their way around. Places need to be memorable, easy to understand, and navigable: the quality known as *legibility*. Legible places offer strong support for understanding their sense, their place identity, as they are closely linked to the *distinctiveness* dimension of identity. These four dimensions of responsiveness—permeability, vitality, variety, and legibility—contribute to users' choices, and therefore to their sense of empowerment. Only places that have a strong sense of empowerment will be read by their users as their own; such places will therefore have a strong sense of place identity. Various qualities of responsiveness, and therefore of a sense of empowerment, are articulated through those spatial and building form typologies defined by the Joint Centre for Urban Design as the Admirable Types of Responsive Environments.[10] These types interact with each other, at different morphological levels, and they define aspects of place identity.

Cultural landscapes that last for a long time show that they are loved and able to meet varying needs over time. Such places offer a great sense of *rootedness*, another dimension important in the place-identity construction. This is particularly important in today's fast-developing world, where cultural landscapes are replicated across the globe. The place that has a strong sense of rootedness will be distinctive and different from other places, and it will also support different cultural interpretations appropriate to a range of different communities.

Cultural landscapes also have important roles to play in fostering perceptions of community membership. Most community memberships are geographically and culturally bound. In today's multicultural societies, an important aspect of place identity is what the German philosopher Wolfgang Welsch calls *transculturality*.[11] Transculturality offers a way of thinking about places at all physical scales, and inclusive of all cultural groups. Transculturality is sometimes difficult for planners and designers to address because it depends on an understanding of, and a feeling for, a range of imagined communities.[12] Some communities are geographically bound; others are constructed in our minds, through community membership. Persons of differing age groups, genders, religions, or cultural backgrounds are likely to generate different community associations. The more we share urban memories and attach positive meanings to particular places, the greater will be our associations of place identity in our memories. Using the concept of transculturality in the design process requires the development of new, more open, co-creative approaches to the design process itself— approaches in which users will be regarded as collaborative experts.

The art of place-making also has important implications for the way we relate to the natural world and to the broad spectrum of natural systems. According to some theorists, we need to think of nature as part of our own culture.[13] Personal and social identities that can be constructed free from the traditional human/nature dichotomy, and cultural landscapes that can support such a construction, are essential to developing an optimistic approach to designing cities and places. Potentially, therefore, it seems that there might be kinds of planning and urban design approaches that have important roles to play in forming cultural landscapes in which people from different imagined communities might live together harmoniously.

To summarize, there are four key issues in the relationship among cultural landscapes, the art of positive place-making, and the construction of positive place identities. First, people need places that will support the most open possible range of choices in people's everyday lives, and that will help us develop the sense of empowerment needed to take advantage of these opportunities. Second, people need landscapes to support the construction of imagined communities rooted in broader cultural landscapes. Third, we need landscapes to help us, as members of particular imagined communities, to develop open, optimistic identities, if we are to find ways of living with others sustainably. Fourth, we need landscapes that will encourage the capacity to live in harmony with the wider ecosystems we call nature. But what does all this mean in practice? How can we design such places?

ANGELL TOWN

The best way to illustrate a well-structured approach to the art of place-making and the creation of positive place identities and local distinctiveness is through a case study of planning and urban design that has addressed these issues in practice. Overall, the case study uses the conceptual framework of empowerment, rootedness, transculturality, and co-dwelling with nature, as a format through which the place is designed and experienced, enabling exploration of the successive emergence of significant new approaches to achieving place identity by design. If we go back to David Novitz's idea of

participatory art and collaborative engagement, it is useful to briefly
discuss how planners, urban designers, and users have engaged collaboratively in developing ideas around issues of place identity. The
case study is the author's own urban design experience, carried out
in collaboration with colleagues from Oxford Brookes University,
local residents of Angell Town, and many otherplayers, including
politicians and builders. This case study also demonstrates how rundown and unloved places can be turned around through a collaborative process of place-making. By *collaborative art of place-making*
is meant here the kind of performance art, as in an orchestra, where
many players engage in a creative performance. In this case, the creative art performance is the shaping of cities and local urban areas
that produce places that are emotionally charged and where the
sense of place is rediscovered.

Angell Town is located in Brixton, in the London Borough of
Lambeth, which lies south of the river Thames. Originally, Angell
Town estate was developed by the Lambeth Architects' Department
during the 1970s to house some four thousand residents. The estate
was showcased at that time as an innovative design concept that
merited its award-winning status in terms of its architectural design
principles. The original estate's morphology, conceived during the
1960s, represented a shift away from high-rise modernist blocks to
more traditional street-orientated layouts. The overall plan was
based on a grid geometry of a perimeter block structure, but with
the segregation of pedestrian and vehicular movements. Elevated
pedestrian access routes, or "pedways" (referred to as "streets in the
sky"), led to individual apartments, and buildings were connected
by bridges. The building typology consisted primarily of four- to
five-story dwellings of either single-story apartments or two-story
maisonettes. Ground floor spaces were designed to accommodate
cars, but there were no other amenities on the estate.

1970s housing, Angell Town.

When the first residents moved in, they were very pleased with their new accommodations. Yet, within a few years, problems began. Some were linked to the poor quality of construction, resulting in water penetration, the breakdown of the central heating system, and other deficiencies. However, the most apparent problem, from the residents' point of view, was the overall spatial layout of the estate, consisting of a poorly connected public space network, with many access routes that separated most users from the rest of Brixton. It was like a gated community. This brought about many unsurveilled public spaces, with no "eyes on the street," to use Jane Jacobs's concept.[14] Apartments, pedways, and deck access corridors had no windows facing the public domain, and residents noticed that there was generally a lack of human contact along these corridors. Some residents observed that the spaces resembled prisons, with apartment doors hidden behind recessed entrances. "In ordinary houses, you can see people in the street through the kitchen window, so there is a chance to see what is going on, and maybe say 'Hi' if you want to—but we soon found out you can't do that here," said one resident during one of the workshop sessions.[15] This building typology, with apartments raised above the ground level, also influenced the parents not to let their children play at the ground level, so children used the bridges to play their games.

Such spatial segregation started to attract unwanted visitors, and the first signs of crime and vandalism began to appear. To reduce the crime on the estate, the police advised, it would be better to demolish the connecting bridges, so that criminals could not escape so easily. Once these bridges were removed, another set of problems began to appear. First, it became more difficult for residents to dispose of rubbish, and unwanted waste was left in hidden corners of the pedways and other dark and unsurveilled spaces; very soon, odors and vermin started to be noticed by the residents. Meanwhile, particularly problematic were the empty ground-level garages that provided hidden and unsurveilled areas for nearby gangs engaged in drug dealing, prostitution, and other crimes.

Other problems were sociocultural, as many residents were unemployed and suffered from health and drug abuse problems. With a very poor management structure in place at that time, and the local estate management department behind with maintenance and repair work, by the mid-1980s, the estate was declared unfit to live in and those who were able to moved to better housing estates in other parts of London. The newspaper reports referred to Angell Town as a "Hell Town." After the violent riots of 1986, the remaining residents decided to take charge of the estate, and in 1987 a group of residents, led by Dora Boatemah, set up the Angell Town Community Project (ATCP).

The newly formed ATCP team found an empty flat on the estate, appropriated it for a headquarters, and began to work on a number of small initiatives. Very soon the residents realized that the task was too big to handle on their own, and they approached the Oxford Brookes Urban Design team (then known as the Oxford Polytechnic Urban Regeneration Consultancy unit) for advice. A collaborative partnership between the Angell Town Community Project and the Oxford Brookes Urban Regeneration Consultancy unit began in 1987. As a starting point, it was important to establish what was wrong with the estate, in urban design terms, and then to generate ideas on how to turn it around. The goal: make Angell Town a place with decent homes and with safe, open spaces and streets for children and residents. The Oxford Brookes team adopted a collaborative two-expert partnership approach. Local residents were the experts on what worked or did not work on the estate; the Oxford Brookes team had the expertise about place-making and understood what was achievable in urban design and architectural terms.[16] The overall working philosophy was based on the art of collaborative engagement.

First, the Oxford Brookes team started with a blank sheet of paper, trying to identify what was seen as problematic by the residents of the estate. This generated all sorts of cascading topics and issues, from unsurveilled spaces to bad housing situations. Some residents were concerned that there was too much dog fouling, which led to the observation that there were too many dogs, which led to a discussion noting that dogs were needed to protect the residents, as they felt unsafe walking through the estate. Very soon, we were able to translate these observations into urban design problems, largely linked to the unsafe spaces resulting from the poor layout of the estate. Second, the residents observed that the building typology was problematic. Their homes, they noted, looked "institutional" and "prison like," not like proper homes. Third, open spaces were neglected and full of rubbish and unwanted furniture. Fourth, and above all, the residents wanted a different kind of place identity.

Once the problems were identified, they were translated into urban design issues and the design team could start addressing them. A number of workshops were organized to explore in more detail how to start the process of new place-making. Discussions with the core group of residents led to the formulation of a survey designed to seek views from the whole populace of the estate, not only from a small group. The survey had to be jargon-free, with complex urban design concepts translated into ordinary English. The core residents' group was very instrumental in designing the survey, so that no errors were made. Given the multicultural composition of the residents, and the fact that some residents were new immigrants (residents came from a variety of countries) and perhaps could not speak English, the survey was translated into many languages and dialects. The residents of the estate were also trained to carry out surveys so that they could assume ownership of their project. Each household, in a total of 820 flats, was approached by a team of local residents, and some two thousand responses were collected and analyzed by the Oxford team.

Two of the major concerns established through these surveys were to overcome the "ghetto" effect of the estate's layout, which separated it from its wider context, and to change the institutional-looking buildings into state-of-the-art, contemporary-styled homes that would attract architectural awards and thus turn the once negative reviews into positive ones. However, the residents also wanted refurbished or new buildings to be seen as part of Brixton, not as some "anywhere" place. The residents identified local streets with beautiful Georgian houses and took the design team there to show what kind of local identity would be appropriate. However, they did not want a mere copy of the past but, rather, buildings that would reflect the rooted nature of the area while also being modern and progressive. Modern-looking buildings, the residents thought, would also be more inclusive of the many cultural groups that lived on the estate. Exploratory, collaborative design workshops were run in the evenings to attract as many local people as possible.

The art of place-making began to take shape by using large-scale three-dimensional models and visual sources, photographs and sketches, that could be understood by all participants. Exhibition panels were placed in the local community center so that residents could make further comments on the presented ideas. The final outcome of these workshops and exhibitions was the forging of a common vision expressing an idea of a new place, a new place identity.

Given the size of the challenge, it was important to achieve a small success so that residents did not get disillusioned. A modest project was implemented that turned a rundown piece of land into a play area for three- to five-year-old children, popularly called "Little Angels." This small initiative also attracted some older children to participate in contributing visions and design ideas. A summer school program was organized for teenagers of the estate to design their own open spaces and play areas. Residents' and young peoples' ideas were later translated into an urban design brief to attract reputable architects, chosen by the residents, as clients, to deliver what residents wanted. The key principle was a new spatial integration at the ground level to improve the natural surveillance and the overall perception of safety across the estate. Second, the brief suggested how the overall integration of the estate could be linked with the wider community of Brixton, avoiding the feel of a ghetto. Third, ideas were proposed for how ground-floor empty garages could be incorporated into refurbished buildings or be used for local community facilities and enterprise units. In order to avoid similar mistakes from the past, different parts of the regeneration scheme were later commissioned to different architects.

The first stage of the project focused on formulating a pilot scheme, during the 1990s, to see how some of the new ideas could work in practice. The ATCP commissioned Burrell-Foley Fisher, a reputable firm of architects, while still retaining the Oxford Brookes Regeneration unit as the urban design advisors. The pilot scheme included the refurbishment of forty-four dwellings, ranging from two-bedroom apartments to seven-bedroom houses (for larger, extended families). The collaborative process of the art of place-making continued through this stage of the detailed work, and residents collaborated in developing ideas for their new dwellings, using large scale models and other visualization techniques. Once the pilot project was completed, with much praise from the residents, politicians, professionals and others, the rest of the estate began to be transformed. Some of the worst blocks were demolished and replaced by state-of-the-art buildings—which have won many awards.

The new, evolving place identity is now celebrated in many ways. First, a sense of empowerment is being achieved by having an integrated spatial structure that connects the estate with its surrounding neighborhoods, and also connects the street system within the estate. This is particularly evident in the elimination of the pedways and their unsafe "streets in the sky," as well as at the ground level of connectivity, with shops and other services taking the place of dark, unsurveilled garages. The residents claim that the overall street layout now supports a much higher degree of legibility, which has improved the overall perception of safety. At the building typology level, new or refurbished townhouses and apartments reflect both a sense of rootedness and transculturality: rootedness is obvious in the way that the parti- or façade composition of Georgian Brixton townhouses has been reflected in the new building typology, and the buildings' contemporary appearance reflects the new and evolving transcultural composition of the residents. For their part, the residents perceive these buildings as distinctly their own.

Positive place identity is also addressed in the detailed design of public open spaces, based on the visions created by the local

New residences, Angell Town.

New residences and playground, Angell Town.

children and the residents, and refined and implemented by Planet Earth, a professional team of landscape designers.

Key features are low walls constructed of crushed concrete from razed buildings on the estate, bound into wire cages of steel rods to form retaining walls. These caged walls, known as *gabions,* express the story of empowerment of local residents and their triumph in achieving a more positive and forward-looking estate. The gabions also bring strong associations of the importance of co-dwelling with nature.

New public spaces, Angell Town.

In conclusion, several key lessons can be drawn. First, the case study interpretations have shown that the conceptual frameworks of empowerment, rootedness, transculturality, and co-dwelling with nature are useful dimensions in the place-identity interpretations and in planning and design of settlements, buildings, and open spaces. Second, it is important to engage with the local users and builders in participatory and collaborative art practices so that places created reflect a greater sense of ownership and therefore of place identity. Such places are also more likely to engender respect for others, and to promote transculturality where different groups and local craftspersons have collaboratively participated in creating their own sense of community and of identity.

This is not to say that these are the only dimensions of place identity that matter. Different contexts may require other dimensions and approaches, particularly when it comes to large-scale new development schemes where the users are absent from the collaborative practice and where other concepts and tools may be necessary. Yet the work at Angell Town holds hope for reclaiming, sustaining, and revitalizing our urban neighborhoods.

NOTES

1. Georgia Butina Watson and Ian Bentley, *Identity by Design* (Oxford: Architectural Press, 2007).

2. Michael Hough, *Out of Place: Restoring Identity of the Cultural Landscape* (New Haven, Conn.: Yale University Press, 1990), 2.

3. Ibid., 3.

4. Chris Abel, *Architecture and Identity: Responses to Cultural and Technological Change,* 2nd ed. (Oxford: Architectural Press, 2000).

5. Watson, *Identity by Design.*

6. Scott Lash, *Another Modernity, A Different Rationality* (Oxford: Blackwell, 1999), 85–86.

7. David Novitz, "Participatory Art and Appreciative Practice," *Journal of Aesthetics and Art Criticism* 59, no. 2 (Spring 2001): 153–166.

8. Watson, *Identity by Design,* 6.

9. See *Responsive Environments: A Manual for Designers,* ed. Ian Bentley (London: Architectural Press, 1985).

10. Ian Bentley et al., *Responsive Environments: Lecture Notes,* 2007.

11. Wolfgang Welsch, *Undoing Aesthetics* (London: Sage, 1997).

12. Benedict Anderson, *Imagined Community, Reflections on the Origin and Spread of Nationalism* (London: Verso, 1983).

13. Adrian Franklin, *Nature and Society Theory* (London: Sage, 2002).

14. Jane Jacobs, *The Death and Life of Great American Cities* (New York: Penguin Books, 1961).

15. Georgia Butina Watson and Ian Bentley, *The Angell Town Workshop,* 1987.

16. Watson, *Identity by Design.*

BEYOND BOUNDARIES

Mo Zell

Andrea Kahn, in "Defining Urban Sites," contrasts the urban boundary conditions of a sixteenth-century sketch of Milan by Leonardo da Vinci to an historical eighteenth-century plan depicting an ideal Renaissance plan of Palmanuova. The Renaissance plan has a clear edge delineated by a heavy defensive boundary wall, while the Leonardo sketch has no clearly defined boundaries or edges. Although these two images convey different notions of representation (the former image is a plan, the latter an evocative sketch illustrating Leonardo's imagined Milan), they reveal an important condition regarding the nature of boundaries. Kahn states "in Leonardo's image no border divides site from situation."[1] There are two key components to this statement: one is the definition of the site by a boundary itself; the second is how that notion of site cannot be divorced from the activity, context, or network defined as the situation. By not limiting a site to a given political, legal (parcel), social, economic, or physical boundary, opportunities for a design's expanded "spatial extension" can occur at a variety of scales.[2]

Boundaries are often equated with a "line of separation." Inherent in Leonardo's sketch and Kahn's description is that demarcations of a site limit the intrinsic connections among disparate elements within the public realm. Therefore, the notion that a site is delineated by a series of edges is limiting and should not serve as the sole definition. By considering a site as boundless, a design intervention can operate at many scales. This essay examines bauenstudio's design of the Northeastern University Veterans Memorial at a variety of operational scales. Kahn suggests that the distinction between site and situation is a relational construct, and for the memorial it is one that relies on a multitude of contexts including landscape, infrastructure, and urban.

In making connections between site and situation while simultaneously being a specific place, the Veterans Memorial employs the language of landscape as an urban design tool, expanding on the notion of landscape urbanism, as elucidated by Charles Waldheim's statement that "landscape has become both the lens through which the contemporary city is represented and the medium through which it is constructed."[3] Waldheim and other supporters of landscape urbanism tenets promote an engagement with infrastructure, blurred boundaries, and the indeterminacy of space that allows for multiple uses on a single site. Through this lens, one experiences the city, and thus the Northeastern University (NEU) Veterans Memorial, as flux with an interweaving of social, physical, and cultural possibilities.

In 2005, Northeastern University announced an *"ideas"* competition to design a memorial to honor approximately four hundred alumni who had died while serving in the U.S. military. The design competition committee selected a small site on campus and provided few limitations to the memorial design; bauenstudio submitted the winning entry. Experience of the site, its surroundings and location, and its relation to the city influenced the memorial design. The memorial was not only considered as a place of remembrance but also as an opportunity to influence the public realm.

BOUNDLESS SITE

The campus of Northeastern University has edges that are not well defined. It merges with three adjacent neighborhoods: the South End, the Fenway, and Mission Hill. The edges of the campus are porous and allow for pedestrian traffic to and through these adjoining neighborhoods. The memorial design capitalizes on the quality of this porosity, including the transitory nature of the population, and the movement of people toward and along the site.

In the early 1980s, the Northeastern campus was covered with a series of parking lots. As a way to cleanse the memory of that condition (and perhaps influenced by Olmsted's nearby Back Bay Fens), the university's landscape architects created a series of curved, meandering pathways edged with trees, shrubs, and flowers. This effort to "overgreen" the campus pushed the buildings into a position of backdrop with layered landscape in front. Unfortunately, the newly employed landscape was relegated to a neutral position within the spaces of the campus, as mere decoration. The university's landscape architects focused on making brick-lined pathways through the campus, while diluting all notions of identity and place.

In designing the NEU Veterans Memorial, bauenstudio considered the existing site a residual one, a formless remnant that resulted from the construction of nearby buildings. The wedge-shaped site described in the competition brief was surrounded by an academic building, a city street, and a brick-paved pedestrian campus path. Its residual nature was reinforced by an existing circular pedestrian pathway within a nondescript plot of grass. A wooden gazebo on the site provided a symbol of domesticity that perversely contradicted the institutional nature of the campus. The existing landscape mirrored that of a typical suburban office park, with discrete areas of "pretty" flowers, grass, and trees. These natural elements provided a manicured buffer between pedestrians and academic buildings, but nothing more.

Expanding on Kahn's notion of spatial extension, the memorial possesses strong tectonic and landscape forms reaching beyond its physical boundaries into the adjacent campus and neighborhoods. The design takes advantage of the motion of pedestrians coming from adjacent areas to and through the site. In this, it calls to mind landscape urbanist principles. The renowned architectural and urban theorist Ignasi Solà-Morales makes a distinction between motion and movement: "To speak of motion rather than movement is to centre our attention on the very action of moving, in its temporal unfolding, rather than on the substantive translation of that action into a generic and abstract concept."[4] Thus, action or motion is elevated to the role of design strategy. The pedestrian is elevated to client, and is visually and physically engaged with the memorial by the nature of its location and flexible spaces.

The site for the memorial encompassed areas beyond the immediate property line including the existing train lines operating to the east, two major pedestrian pathways crisscrossing at the site, the intimate nature of the adjacent city street connected to a major city thoroughfare, and a number of vertical surfaces defined by adjacent academic buildings. Additionally, bauenstudio considered the nature of this site culturally within the context of a university and an urban campus, visibly available to the university community, neighborhood community, and commuters using the public train line. (The train station housed stops for the regional commuter rail as well as the local orange line of the "T" and served as a connection to local attractions including the Museum of Fine Arts, Fenway Park, and the Isabella Stewart Gardner Museum.) As happens with many landscape urbanism projects, engagement with existing infrastructural elements, like the train, became important to the design. By acknowledging the location, temporality, and number of persons using the train, the siting of the memorial wall capitalizes on these existing conditions so as to have the greatest impact on multiple constituents. Through the process of defining the site with multiple overlapping boundaries established by multiple situations—site, campus neighborhood, district, city, and region—and multiple users, a framework for design was established. Although the scale of the actual design intervention is relatively small, through the implementation of multiple boundaries, the memorial operates within a larger "scale of influence," magnifying the opportunity for spatial extension.

Expanding on Linda Pollak's notion of the constructed ground as a "hybrid framework . . . [that] invests in the ground itself as a material for design, using landscape as both a structuring element and a medium for rethinking urban conditions,"[5] bauenstudio repudiated any notion of a fixed perception of a boundary or edge. Strategically deployed hardscape and softscape landscape materials constructed the ground to create distinct areas of gathering, weaving vertical landscape and architectural elements to blur spatial distinctions and develop a rich spatial ambiguity. The ambiguity of edge conditions between landscape elements allows a multiplicity of readings at a variety of scales for the public and private spaces. An underlying grid structure organizes and unites the natural and constructed elements of design. This four-foot grid serves as a counterpoint to the meandering paths and buildings that pervade the campus. Within the grass appears a series of four-inch granite strips. These strips extend beyond the immediate site, beyond the red-twig dogwood edge, into the adjacent grove of trees. Although visually disconnected by the three-foot-high dogwoods, the ground plane is meant to be understood as a single connected canvas, extending one space into another.

Granite and bluestone pavers (hardscape) indicate public access for gathering and movement. Again, there are clear material

Aerial view showing blurred boundaries between the public path and
memorial public space (foreground), as well as the hardscape of the
ceremonial space and the softscape of the contemplative space. Photo by
Mark Roehrle, bauenstudio.

distinctions between two different public gathering spaces, but
spatially they overlap with one another and with the adjacent
pedestrian pathways. Additional material changes at the edge of
the public space, the weaving of the brick pavers of the pedestrian
network with newly laid concrete pavers, reinforces the ambiguity
of the two spaces, denying any sense of boundary of the site.

Grass (softscape) is used in the private, contemplative space as a
surface material. It is a familiar, domestic material, yet in this application it can be interpreted as inaccessible. A granite hardscape
edges the grass on two sides to limit overuse by the public. The granite isolates the grass area by creating a series of walkable surfaces
around the grass. Material changes separate the contemplative
area from the adjacent public area, but spatially they are connected.

At the surface of the ground, a clear edge is defined where the hardscape meets the softscape, but physically there is no spatial boundary separating them. The grass area is also bounded to the north with a granite bench. The bench is a strong, low horizontal element that dilutes the sense of boundary inferred by the transition from one material to another. That is, the forty-foot bench overlaps both the bluestone pavers of the public entry court and the grass of the contemplative space. This overlap blurs the boundaries of the spaces and allows for flexibility of uses. In addition, the lowness of the bench provides porosity to the north.

The vertical landscape elements on the site act as edges but not boundaries. This is achieved through placement and scale. For instance, upon crossing the public entry court, the memorial wall is seen to mark an edge to the contemplative space but, since it also sits in a central position between the adjacent buildings, this "edgeness" is diluted. The memorial wall is simultaneously edge and center. As Kahn states, "site boundaries shift in relationship to the position— the physical location and ideological stance—of their beholder."[6] By acknowledging multiple approach conditions, along with positioning the memorial wall at a major pedestrian intersection on campus (the crossing of those departing from the train with local student traffic), the boundaries of the memorial are constantly changing. Establishing this openness on all sides of the memorial reinforces a nonhierarchical condition.

SITUATION: THE HUMAN PERSPECTIVE

Camillo Sitte, a nineteenth-century urban designer and theorist, described the urban fabric as a sequence of constantly changing framing devices to engage the viewer. Sitte advocated for visual and artistic effects throughout the city. He observed, "it was not enough that the

production of effects in theater scenery be cherished as an art in itself;
the architect was also supposed to position his buildings, colonnades,
monuments, fountains, obelisks and the like according to the same
rules."[7] He stated, "What counts is the position of the spectator and
the direction in which he is looking."[8] Sitte relied on the pedestrian,
the pedestrian's scale relative to the adjacent context, and the rate of
movement as the primary considerations in urban design.

Southern view. Pedestrian view from the train station to the public side of
the memorial wall. Digital image by bauenstudio.

To engage the pedestrian spectator as well as spatially extend the
site, bauenstudio utilized a system of views to locate the main program elements on the site. The construct of views into the site helps
orchestrate a visual sequence within the campus to create connections between the moving observer and landscape, between circula-
tion and place. These views ensure that the spaces are balanced
between being visually protective and being appropriately open for

a variety of activities, including ceremonial events. One of the main benefits to employing this design strategy is that the perception of space extends the site beyond the limitations of the property, blurring any notion of a site boundary; the indeterminacy of the space allows for multiple readings of this site.

Western view of overlapping and contemplative spaces. Photo by bauenstudio.

Along the four main axes into the site, aligned with the cardinal points, pedestrian views establish the layout of the memorial, including the wall location, the orientation of the wall on the site, and the dispersal of the programmatic elements of the memorial. This application of perspective establishes the importance of the pedestrian within the urban context. Thus, views present a visual intention, while framing devices provide the means of implementation. Framing devices bound the field of vision from the general to the particular. These include existing building facades, cornices, plantings, walls, and trees.

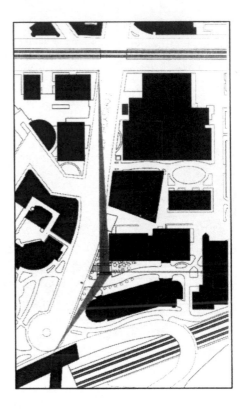

Local situation and
spatial extension diagram.
Digital image by
bauenstudio.

The northern view is established by the understory of the tree
canopy and the surface of the granite bench. These framing devices
provide a threshold for viewing into the memorial site, with an
emphasis on the private side of the memorial wall. The tree canopy
obscures the building beyond the site, emphasizing the contemplative garden and commemorative wall.

The eastern view into the site, accessed mainly by the campus community, is framed by the edge of a newly planted tree grove, organized
linearly, and the edge of the memorial wall itself. An allée of birch
trees frame the narrow space where the visitor interacts with the wall.
This limited view is terminated, in the distance, by two flagpoles.

The southern view, the main view for commuters departing the train station, utilizes an academic building in the foreground and a new grouping of trees to frame the public side of the memorial wall. In this instance, non-coplanar elements, elements offset from one another in three-dimensional space, operate as framing devices.

The western view, the main entry into the site from the street, is framed by two large trees and reinforced by the low granite bench and the memorial wall. The cornice lines of the adjacent buildings, flanking the memorial site, define a larger space in which the memorial is situated and viewed. This western view is terminated by a series of layered, vertical landscape elements at the horizon, along with hard and softscape elements on the ground plane. The vertical layers consist of red-twig dogwoods and a grove of birch trees; the ground is covered with bluestone and grass.

By engaging framing devices off the site, the memorial extends its presence beyond the official boundaries of the site. Significant, yet small, interventions like this memorial can assert themselves into a variety of scaled situations in such a manner as to command a more prominent position. By reclaiming this site from a residual condition, the memorial establishes overlapping public spaces that provide opportunities for the campus community and the general public to gather in, occupy, and transmute space into place. The views establish the spatial extension into the adjacent context, and the indeterminacy of spaces provides the freedom for a variety of experiences, responses, and interactions within the site.

Public and Private Remembrance

The memorial, considered within the context of a sacred place on a campus, and within the broader context of commemoration and memorial design, features an official commemoration, a laser-etched mural depicting iconic images from five wars. These scenes have been modified and abstracted into pixilated images. Viewed from afar, the pixilated images are clear, but as one approaches, the images dissolve and have an ethereal effect. Thus, these visual images on the wall operate at a multitude of scales engaging the pedestrian network at both close range and from a distance.

The private northern side of the wall, however, is the focal point of remembrance for the memorial. It reflects the vernacular or personal commemoration, the intimate nature of war and loss. On this side of the wall are 279 stainless steel plates. From a distance, their collective appearance speaks to an enduring bond of soldiers in battle. When viewed at close range, each plate is inscribed with a soldier's name, rank, hometown, birth and death dates, college major, and graduation year. These symbolic "dog tags" are designed to be touched and held. They are more than mere record, for, to the living, they say, "This is my brother, my son, my father, my friend." From far and near, through both a visual and a tactile connection, for those close to and remote from the event, the Veterans Memorial offers solace, honor, and respite.

The memorial employs materials and spaces in ways that deconstruct any notion of a singular boundary on the site. The design embraces a multiplicity of readings at many scales while engaging multiple constituencies. Although funded by Northeastern, its location along pedestrian arteries provides opportunities for diverse social groups to use the spaces. Landscape here has allowed creation of truly public rather than privatized spaces. By designing a memorial using the language of landscape to interact with many urban conditions, bauenstudio foregrounded landscape as a unique opportunity for engaging the dynamic potential of the contemporary city. Stan Allen, as quoted in Waldheim's essay "Landscape as Urbanism" in this volume, states, "Landscape has traditionally been

Name plates on the Veterans Memorial. Photo by bauenstudio.

defined as the art of organizing horizontal surfaces. . . . By paying close attention to these surface conditions—not only configuration, but also materiality and performance—designers can activate space and produce urban effects without the weighty apparatus of traditional space making."[9] In keeping with Allen's notion of landscape's role in shaping the contemporary city and Kahn's sense of spatial extension, the Northeastern University Veterans Memorial extends its spatial influence beyond its site into the adjoining campus and urban context by engaging pedestrian users through consciously placed landscape elements.

NOTES

1. Andrea Kahn, "Defining Urban Sites," in *Site Matters: design concepts, histories, and strategies,* ed. Carol J. Burns and Andrea Kahn (New York: Routledge, 2005), 284.

2. Kahn explains spatial extension as many scales operating simultaneously on a particular urban site. Scales are multiple-sized networks. Burns identifies these for Times Square as the local, global, metropolitan and regional scale.

3. Charles Waldheim, "A Reference Manifesto," in *The Landscape Urbanism Reader,* ed. Charles Waldheim (New York: Princeton Architectural Press, 2006), 15.

4. Ignasi Solà-Morales, "Present and Futures. Architecture in Cities," in *Present and Futures: Architecture in Cities,* ed. Ignasi Solà-Morales and Xavier Costa, trans. Mark Woudby (Barcelona: ACTAR, 1996), 14.

5. Linda Pollak, "Constructed Ground: Questions of Scale," in *Landscape Urbanism Reader,* ed. Waldheim, 127.

6. Kahn, *Site Matters,* 292.

7. Camillo Sitte, *The Birth of Modern City Planning,* trans. George Collins and Christiane Crasemann (New York: Rizzoli, 1986), 124.

8. Ibid., 217.

9. Stan Allen, "Landscape as Urbanism," in *Landscape Urbanism Reader,* ed. Waldheim, 37.

PART III

URBAN PERCEPTIONS

TIGERS, TRICKSTERS, AND OTHER URBAN LEGENDS

CHINESE CITIES

DESIGN AND DISAPPEARANCE

Ackbar Abbas

THE CHINESE CITY

As a way of "envisioning the urban," let us, first, list six characteristics of the Chinese city today found almost everywhere. The first characteristic is a certain operatic quality. In the Chinese Sichuan Opera, there is a secret technique known as "changing face," or *bian lian,* where the actor changes one painted face for another with a quick turn of the head. There is something of this "changing face" effect when we look at the changing space of the Chinese city. We see the transformations, but we cannot believe our eyes or our ears when we hear the famous formulation, usually attributed to Deng, "to get rich is glorious." The formulation sounds more like a magic formula than a political party slogan; it sounds more operatic than pragmatic. To see the Chinese city, then, as operatic, rather than as the result of solely pragmatic decisions, opens up the analysis and allows us to give some weight to factors other than the economic.

The operatic city is also an anticipatory city: this is a second characteristic of the Chinese city. We see the anticipatory in phenomena of empty residential and commercial buildings in Shanghai (or in the destruction of the *hutongs* in Beijing, its traditional narrow-laned neighborhoods) that make way for the construction of miles and miles of new mall spaces, even before the businesses are there to fill them. These actions have been explained as instances of speculative overbuilding and overpricing, or of administrative bungling and red tape, but they can also be seen as instances of anticipatory practices. Anticipation differs from speculation, in that speculation has an eye on the market, while anticipation displays a certain indifference to the market. And the most intense anticipation of all is the as yet unfounded conviction that the twenty-first century will someday become the Chinese century.

Exactly because anticipation is not based on anything provable or definitive, the anticipatory city is subject to mood swings, and this is a third characteristic of the Chinese city: it is a manic-depressive city. Such cities are never simply interesting or boring; rather, moments of heightened intensity and exhilaration alternate with moments of withdrawal and apathy. Paradoxically, what created the manic-depressive city was the decentralization of state control over the running of cities, which gave rise to so many great expectations in the first place. However, decentralization never meant the absence of control, only a different form of control. So, while the state encourages or at least allows many grandiose projects to be launched, it also demands that they be sifted through bureaucratic channels. It is a similar story when we turn from the market to the arts. The new television producers on Chinese Central Television (CCTV), who are today trained professionals and not bureaucrats, may be genuinely interested in promoting innovative cultural programs free of clichés and propaganda, but the work they commission can be censored, at any time and without explanation, by the higher administration. It is this constant oscillation, at all levels of urban life, between permissiveness and prohibition that helps create the manic-depressive city.

Even after the introduction of the so-called open-door policy and decentralization, the Chinese city is hardly an open city in the liberal sense, though it is by no means as totalitarian as hostile critics describe. Differences are allowed to surface—in fashions, lifestyles, sexual preferences—but, generally speaking, differences are not valued for their own sake, but rather are exploited, as in arbitrage. The Chinese city as arbitrage city: this is its fourth characteristic. The term *arbitrage* comes from economics, and it refers to the way profits are obtained by capitalizing, through the use of electronic technologies, on small differences in the price of stocks and currencies in different parts of the world and in different time zones. The models for arbitrage city are the stock market and the currency exchange. Technology and information take on the central roles, shaping the experience of the city as an experience of speed, virtuality, and real time. In short, arbitrage city is the moment when the Chinese city goes global, and going along with it are strange new politico-economic forms, like "the socialist market economy," and new urban forms, like the Special Economic Zones (SEZs), the Special Administrative Regions (SARs), and megacities, formed through combining existing cities into so-called metropolitan interlocking regions (MIRs), like the Hong Kong-Macau-Shenzhen-Zhuhai-Guangzhou conurbation on the Pearl River Delta, already described as "the megalopolis with Chinese characteristics."[1]

A fifth characteristic of the Chinese city is the appearance of a new kind of operator, both in the colloquial sense of someone who acts out of self-interest in a manipulative way, and in the mathematical sense of a function that symbolizes how an operation works. The new Chinese city has given rise to new operators in this double sense. Operators include: business people with private capital, foreign investors, municipal authorities who as a result of decentralization have a certain newfound autonomy in running the city, and the state itself, which, throughout the reform process, has not stopped being a player. What all these operators have in common is the spirit of entrepreneurship, so that the operator of operators is the figure of the entrepreneur, who has now replaced the revolutionary worker as the ideal type. The entrepreneur characterizes the Chinese city in the same way that the *flâneur*, according to Walter Benjamin, characterized the modern European city. In his walks around the city, the flâneur collected stories to sell to newspapers and tabloids. His medium was print. By contrast, the entrepreneur lives in an age of electronic media. Entrepreneurs are arbitrageurs. Equipped with cell phones, they let their fingers do the walking.

These five characterizations—the operatic city, the anticipatory city, the manic-depressive city, the arbitrage city, and the entrepreneurial city—are admittedly exaggerations, but it seems that, in China today, nothing is true except the exaggerations. These exaggerations evoke one final characterization, the disappearing city, but in a special sense of the word. The city disappears not because we don't see it, but because we don't know what we are seeing. Disappearance is not absence; it is a kind of pathology of presence. More and more, it seems, images of the city show less and less about the city. How much have we learnt about Beijing from watching the Olympics on television? The city disappears, there, not because there is no image of the city but because, in an age of information, there are too many. At the same time, together with this proliferation of city images, and as a necessary accompaniment, we find a radical disconnection between image and city. Thus what is truly remarkable about Rem Koolhaas's CCTV building in Beijing is not, as is sometimes claimed, that it projects in its extraordinary sign some image of the speed of information technologies that is already making cinematic images look passé; what is truly remarkable is why such an ultraconservative institution like CCTV should commission such an ultracontemporary architect to design its headquarters. It is as if what we see had no real relation to what we know, as if—to use

K.'s picturesque terminology—a "lobotomy" has taken place that disconnects the visible from the intelligible, or as if the new image of CCTV were a *Photoshopped* image, where a socialist body is grafted onto a market economy face.

Yet, despite the disconnection, it would be premature to give in to postmodern cynicism. Although images cannot capture the city directly, this fact does not prevent the city from seeping into images and other artifacts when they are not looking. Or, to put it in another way, the city cannot be observed directly, but it can be deduced or envisioned from the effects and distortions it produces, effects and distortions called cinema, architecture, design, new media, and so on. All these cultural practices can also be thought of as *parapraxes:* something like slips of the tongue or other inadvertent mistakes that provide evidence for the existence of what cannot be made evident—the disappearing city.

Perpetual Motion

For an example of this kind of evidence, let us turn now to a film. This film is Ning Ying's *Wu qiong dong*—or, in English, *Perpetual Motion* (2005). Unlike Ning Ying's three previous films (the *Beijing Trilogy*), much of which take place in the streets, *Perpetual Motion* takes place mainly in a *siheyuan,* the Chinese courtyard house, where what Benjamin called the "phantasmagorias of the interior," are played out in the different and highly paradoxical context of the socialist market economy. The title itself alludes to the constant oscillation, the perpetual motion—between permissiveness and prohibition, free agency and control—noted earlier at all levels of life in China today, including affective life.

The film begins as a banal story of adultery. One day Niu Niu, a successful businesswoman stumbles across some steamy erotic

emails her husband received from his secret lover. She believes that
the most likely suspects are La La, an attractive and talented international artist; Mrs.Yeh, a local real estate mogul; and Qin Qin, a former movie star. She invites them to the siheyuan for a Spring
Festival mahjong party, in order to find out who the culprit is. In the
course of the mahjong game, Niu Niu encourages everyone to recall
her personal history, initially with the intention of seeing what each
would give away, but gradually she too joins in. The investigation
morphs into the confessional, and at this point a different note
begins to be heard. As the four characters tell their stories, it is as if
they were collectively trying to locate the particular moment in history when everything changed. So the film's opening question,
"Who is the secret lover?" becomes in the end "How did things, that
is, private and public history, get to be this way?" Ironically, it is Niu
Niu who tells the longest personal story, reminiscing about how she
met her husband, trying to find in the details of their early romance
the seeds of their estrangement.

As important to the story as the four women is the absent figure of
the husband; we only see his photograph, but we never see him
directly. The husband is important as a figure of betrayal—of personal betrayal, obviously, but also as summing up all the uncertain-
ties and betrayals of history culminating in a present-day globalizing
China. A minor crisis of the interior (adultery) becomes the symp-
tom of a larger crisis. This is why his death in a car accident produces,
at the end of the film, a double dénouement. One of the film's questions, "Who is the lover?" is answered. It turns out to be Qin Qin, the
ex-film actress, who breaks down and cries at the news of the husband's death. But the film's other question, "How did things get this
way?" remains suspended in the air. It produces a second dénouement that is both more crucial and less clear-cut than the first. This
dénouement takes the form of a sudden nervous breakdown of La La

the artist, whose hysterical laughter drowns out Qin Qin's senti-
mental sobs: her parents were high officials and loyal Communists
who were nevertheless imprisoned during the Cultural Revolution.

This second dénouement raises more questions than it can
answer. Are we seeing the betrayals of history both at the personal
and political level? We remember how Chinese socialism seduced and
abandoned those most devoted to it, like La La's parents. Or are we
experiencing, in La La's laughter, history-as-hysteria, a confused
occulted history best exemplified in what socialism in China has
become? Because what we are seeing in the socialist market economy is neither the life nor death of socialism, but its afterlife: a
posthumous socialism that can paradoxically have a vitality stronger
than ever, whose twin emblems might be, on the one hand, Mao's
mausoleum where his preserved body (or, some say, a replica) is on
display, and, on the other hand, the urban-planning museums
found in Beijing, Shanghai, and other self-respecting Chinese cities,
where incredibly detailed scale models of the future metropolis are
exhibited. The film ends on a suspended note. We hear the sound of
sirens as an ambulance takes La La away, and we watch the three
other women walk out of the siheyuan into a typical Beijing scene of
construction sites.

DESIGN AND DISAPPEARANCE

The last image in *Perpetual Motion* allows us to move from stories of
damaged lives to stories of damaged cities, cities damaged ironically
from the best of intentions, cities damaged through design. The issue
of cities and the issue of design are clearly among the two most crucial issues for China today. The People's Republic of China came into
existence through the Marxist tactic of using the countryside to
encircle the city. In the present era of economic reform, we are seeing

something like the city's revenge. In 1954, only 13.6 percent of Chinese lived in cities; in 2007, that figure rose to 45 percent. Four hundred new cities with a population of over a million each are planned to materialize by 2020, and almost five hundred million square meters of built space will have been constructed each year between 2000 and 2020.[2] Whether these cities and spaces are being built with 20/20 urban vision is another question.

The issue of design is as crucial and wide-ranging in its implications as the issue of cities. China can now produce goods cheaply and well; it can also copy and replicate designs to perfection. There is a thriving trade in fakes, in spite of membership in the World Trade Organization (WTO), though there are signs that this trade may be abating. However, while the fake industry can be surprisingly innovative, the design of legitimate products still tends to be stiff, conservative, and derivative—for reasons that deserve careful consideration. What is clear is that once China develops a design culture, there will be a good chance that the twenty-first century will indeed be the Chinese century. The stakes are that high.

These two issues come together when we ask what is involved in designing cities that are not only sustainable but also sustaining, able to provide work, pleasure, and challenges, cities that we can love. "Better City, Better Life" is the slogan of Expo 2010 in Shanghai, but the current way of envisioning a better city has produced not better lives but less happy ones. We can surmise that this is the case when we see wave after wave of nostalgia sweeping over China, such as nostalgia for the Cultural Revolution, and, when that abated, nostalgia for the 1980s, the end of the Cultural Revolution. In Beijing and Shanghai in particular, urban design has involved the destruction of the urban fabric and its replacement by "a city of objects"—that is, a city full of iconic buildings designated by foreign brand-name architects, buildings that, like celebrities, are famous for being famous, but that the average citizen finds hard to relate to. One striking case is the magnificent newly completed CCTV building by Rem Koolhaas. When the Mandarin Oriental Hotel attached to it caught fire, many Beijing residents watched it burn down, not with dismay at the destruction of a landmark in a prime area of town, but with a kind of callous satisfaction at seeing a high-flying project grounded, a project that they felt had nothing to do with them in the first place. Chinese urban design has created what Bruno Latour, in a lecture on design, calls "matters-of-fact," not "matters-of-concern."[3] The Chinese city does not address the consensus of its citizens; it has become a playground for European and American architects to realize their urban fantasies, fantasies that are no longer realizable in Europe and America today.

One alternative to the vision of a city of objects, it is often thought, is a concern for preservation. But, interestingly enough, many preservation projects intent on saving historical buildings turn them, in the process, once more into buildings-as-objects. A preserved building is a strange thing: it may look old and familiar but the grids and coordinates by which we understand it have surreptitiously changed. The logic that preservation follows is less a logic of cultural heritage than a logic of global tourism, and this is why it is no contradiction that Shanghai, the city undergoing the most rapid urban development, is also the city most interested in preservation. To say this is in no way to devalue preservation projects, but only to underline the slipperiness of the enterprise: how, in preserving the historic value of a building, we may inadvertently be isolating it from history. Thus, the real preservationist can only be a melancholic: someone who shows us fear in a handful of dust, who presents a preserved building as a handful of historic dust—even before it has crumbled. It is therefore not a question of preserving the hutong against the high-rise, or the bicycle against the motor car. The crucial question is how design can produce matters-of-concern and not just matters-of-fact, in the specific context of the disappearing Chinese city. Let me reiterate that "disappearance" is not absence but a kind of pathology of presence (more "found and lost" perhaps, than "lost and found"). We experience disappearance in the ghostly presence of socialism in the social market economy, in the proliferation of images and Photoshopped images, in a history that is pressing and insistent but occulted, and in cities that have virtually become black holes, whose nature can only be deduced from the often bizarre effects and affects they produce.

The most primitive notion of design is to think of it as adding something to an object without changing it: design as packaging. I presume we can all agree that design can be more than, and other than, this. Hence the opposite notion: to think of design as transformative, and to stress its ability to change culture and society as much as politics and ideology can do. This is a truly seductive notion, epitomized in Le Corbusier's pithy question "Architecture or Revolution?" (a version of "Sophie's choice"). The implication here is that architecture and design obviate the need for revolution, because urban planning can already revolutionize our lives—provided the expert planner is given a free hand, and allowed to act as a kind of benign totalitarian. The problem, though, is that a design that changes our lives can be perceived as *having designs on us,* especially when it is undertaken by lesser designers, like state and city planners. Moreover, it is doubtful whether total design, including Le Corbusier's, ever worked, even when the designer has not been interfered with; it will certainly not work as an approach to the disappearing city, and this brings us to a third notion of design, which we may call "poor design."

Poor design is not bad design, a populist glorification of amateurism. Nor is it just design for the poor, but for everyone. It begins with the growing awareness that what is happening in cities today outpaces urban theory, and that the resources at our disposal are inadequate to our task. But rather than bemoan this fact, it turns inadequacy itself into a source and resource of design: hence, poor/design. Poor design does not entail the abandonment of design or the death of the designer, only the abandonment of hubristically revolutionary notions of design and unfounded notions of the designer as creator. Design is not creation. It does not start from scratch or with tabula rasa. It is not revolutionary but *modestly revisionary,* insofar as it has to start with given objects and situations. It has to start with what is already there. But the task of design in the disappearing city, as we have seen, cannot simply be to look at what is there, because what is there is precisely the problem of disappearances. Rather, the task is to look again at what is not there, or, to put this less glibly, to develop an attentiveness to what else the city can be and let this "what else" guide the design. For Roland Barthes, the city we can love is "the site for our encounter with the other."[4] Barthes's language already sounds old-fashioned, but the sentiment is defensible, even if we note that in some cities "the site of an encounter with the other" is more likely to be a mugging.

NOTES

1. John R. Logan, *The New Chinese City* (Oxford: Blackwell, 2002), 70.

2. Frederic Edelmann, *In the Chinese City* (Barcelona: Actar, 2008), 12–13.

3. Bruno Latour, "A Cautious Prometheus?" (keynote lecture presented at the conference of the Design History Society, Falmouth, England, September 2008).

4. Roland Barthes, "'Semiology and Urbanism," in *Architecture Culture, 1943–1968,* ed. Joan Ockham (New York: Rizzoli, 1993), 417.

FROM "THE DEAD"
TO THE DEAD

THE DISPOSABLE BODIES
AND DISPOSABLE CULTURE OF
CELTIC TIGER NOIR

Andrew Kincaid

Detective Carl McCadden is a lonely man. His wife has just left him. "'I felt like a case you'd solved,'" she explains. "'I was interesting once. Years ago.'" McCadden's mood is black. He's "calmly, almost contentedly, waiting to hit the bottom."[1] It is in the midst of this crisis of alienation and confusion that he's called to investigate a series of brutal murders. Young blond women are turning up dead, beaten beyond recognition. McCadden's investigation draws him into a sordid underworld of prostitution and pornography, drugs and political corruption—the geography of a bleak and segregated city, replete with blind alleys and dark cellar hideouts. McCadden, a sharp-talking tough cop, uncovers a ring of prostitution whose leaders are respectable, powerful citizens; he breaks the case, prevents more innocent young girls from falling into lives of degradation, and, in the process, manages to bring himself halfway back from despair.

Much of this sounds familiar, of course. The language of the hard-boiled detective novel, the imagery of film noir, has been more or less the exclusive domain of one or two American cities—especially Los Angeles, both pre- and post-war, which, with its slippery economy and its new, glossy, superficial culture, was the perfect urban environment for expressing the violence, insecurity, and transformational morality of the time. But McCadden's milieu is Waterford, and Ireland, not America, is now the landscape that is changing. The Celtic Tiger, R.I.P., presented its citizens with equal measures of prosperity, confusion, violence, and hope. Now that the boom economy has officially tanked, the popular, mass-marketed crime paperbacks that became a staple of the Irish literary diet in the 1990s and the early years of the new century have proven to have offered not only a critique of the Tiger years, but also a prescient image of the post-collapse darkness.

A few years ago, Declan Kiberd, writing on the state of contemporary Irish literature, wondered why there seemed no fiction on the newly thriving Irish economy; Kiberd looked at novels about the greed and superficiality of 1980s America, such as *Bonfire of the Vanities* and *Bright Lights, Big City,* and asked why no such literature existed reflecting the similar moment in Ireland. In his essay, Kiberd suggested that the medium best expressing the then-present moment was film.[2] But in fact the Celtic Tiger did produce a literary type that represented the violence, the wealth, the ugliness, the nostalgia, the speed, and the movement inherent in its moment. And the books of this genre are a snapshot of this movement, of the fast pace of cultural change—immigration, growth of attendant cosmopolitanism and racism, massive housing bubble, a newly wealthy, upwardly mobile young workforce—and it is, perhaps, this speed that causes Kiberd to suggest that film would have been an obvious medium to showcase it.

But over the last decade, an interesting new format, perhaps a hybrid of various genres (hard-boiled detective, forensic thriller, crime mystery) has arisen.[3] An interesting feature of this burgeoning genre is that many of these crime novels are written by minor Irish celebrities, a fact that reflects the connection between B-list superficiality and the economic boom that creates it. Liz Allen, the prominent journalist who replaced Veronica Guerin at *The Independent,* has written two novels that focus on strong-minded, beautiful female detectives hired to solve violent crimes against beautiful young women in Dublin.[4] Sean Moncrieff and Gareth O'Callaghan are both political radio talk show hosts. Moncrieff's *Dublin* (2001) is marketed as an Irish version of *Pulp Fiction,* and the plot involves a Russian drug ring whose violence gets unleashed on Bloomsday.[5] Following in the footsteps of classic noir writers, some of these other novelists adopt the serial format, tracking the exploits and personal lives of one detective. Ken Bruen is the standout among these writers, and his protagonist, the Anglo-monikered Jack Taylor, has, for close to a dozen novels, investigated the killing of tinkers and the so-called suicides of teenage girls in Galway. Within the last two years, Bruen has produced several potboilers, including *Priest* (January 2008), *Once Were Cops* (May 2008), and *Sanctuary* (May 2009). Jim Lusby's Carl McCadden series elevates Waterford to the ranks of urban noir. A new writer on the scene, Cormac Millar, a professor of Italian at Trinity, has launched a series of detective novels starring Seamus (Irish for James) Joyce.[6] As you would expect from this genre, several of these pulp fiction thrillers rely also on the trope of the serial killer. Ingrid Black's *The Dead* (2004) focuses on an ex-FBI agent who, at the beginning of the novel, has received communication from a serial killer long thought dead. (By now you may have noticed the Joycean current that runs through many of these books, perhaps in an attempt to add weight to this genre, perhaps an admission of its current tenuous hold on the term *literature.*) The Celtic Tiger may not have produced the high literary format noted in previous eras; it may, in fact, run against the stereotype of Irish cultural production. Undeniably, though, this genre exists, and it is no coincidence that it was born at a time when so much in Ireland was insecure, and that beneath the apparent glamour of a postmodern society lay nostalgia, fear, and violence.

Much, of course, has changed in Ireland recently, and it remains to be seen how this genre, and popular literature generally, will respond to the global financial recession. I suspect that noir will lend itself to this outward despair. As a matter of fact, Irish emigration to London and America has increased recently, a trend many thought was finally behind us.[7] This goes hand in hand with a reported upsurge in a new Irish phenomenon, large-scale regret among those who had returned from the United States and elsewhere, lured back by what they thought would be lasting economic success.[8] Noir proves a perfect genre to capitalize on these undercurrents of hopelessness.

Perhaps the most striking aspect of many of the novels discussed here is the conscious reference to American noir. The features of noir translate particularly well to Ireland at this historical juncture. The most distinguishing feature of the classic noir novel is its representation of the city. The urban world in noir is dark and gloomy. Frequently, the rain pours down, casting an obvious pall on all emotions of the story: the persistent wet and fog reflect the moral corruption of society, which is most often later revealed to have its roots in politicians and the nouveau riche, who have come to their wealth and power dishonestly and now cavort with the criminal element and the underworld. There is an easy movement back and forth between these two milieus. In classic noir, decadence is the problem, and the city is an inhospitable wasteland. It's no wonder, then, that this genre translates to urban Ireland, where the Celtic Tiger produced new wealth, with all its attendant pretensions, criminality,

black economy, and a changing, or at least newly exposed, value system. "Rain was general all over Dublin" in Ingrid Black's *The Dead*.
"It was the first day of December."[9] In Lusby's *Flashback*, Waterford's dockland avenues are "small, musty . . . gloomy . . . chilly . . .
old and worn and neglected. . . . You got the impression it was waiting for night and for darkness."[10] In the Irish version of noir, a case
is not merely a problem, but an opportunity, albeit ultimately a
futile one, to root out evil in the corrupt urban world. *The Dead's*
plot is reminiscent of the movie *Se7en*: a former FBI agent, who has
settled in Dublin, is brought in to help the Irish police capture a
serial killer who leaves his mark on his victims in the form of religious quotations. In Lusby's novel, corruption takes the form of a
pornography ring and the serial murder of young, blond prostitutes.
Ireland's rapid urban expansion led to real-life gang violence, a drug
culture, shady real estate schemes, and police corruption—fertile
ground for the emergence of neo-noir.

The detective, in a classic noir novel, is the moral center of the
story. He is able to balance a code of ethics that is almost nostalgic in
its premodern commitment to honor, with, on the other hand, a
savvy pragmatism that allows him to navigate the shadier contours
of the city's unethical elements. Liz Allen's Deborah Parker, in *The
Last to Know* (2004), holds an unwavering belief in the sanctity of
the justice system, in every accused person's right to a fair trial.[11]
Within that rubric, she has no qualms about visiting Mugsy
Mooney, Dublin's most notorious mob boss, in his posh, tacky suburban home, advising Mooney on how best to cover for his violent
son, a pimp, to prevent him from going to jail, and then accepting a
€20,000 retainer for her legal services. Deborah Parker works in
both worlds. The noir detective moves between the old and the
new, a character of continuity. He (or, occasionally, she) is a com-
forting link between cherished older values and the runaway train of

present-day excess. The particular context of these Irish noir novels points to contemporary discomfort (or, these days, even distress) and the ever-present connection between tradition and modernity. The heroes of these novels not only straddle ethical codes, they seem to walk a line between old Ireland and new Ireland, between thatched cottages and box apartments, between the safety of the knowable community and the random violence of the new city, between familial protectiveness and modern, grown-up independence and alienation. The detective in the Irish noir novel invariably nurses nostalgia for a caring, affectionate parent, but his current state is one of loneliness and anxiety. This condition typifies modernity, and nowhere is this clearer than in the rapidly changing urban environment—today's Ireland.

What is also interesting to note about these novels is that, contrary to age-old stereotypes of a predominantly rural country, now all of Ireland fits the bill for noir. Each of these novels focuses on a different regional urban center, a geographical device that paints a picture of a thoroughly modernizing, modern country. Another bridge these novels build is one between old and new forms of justice. Invariably, the cynical, tough, pragmatic detective is called upon to enact a sort of street justice upon a perpetrator; the novels are sympathetic to this kind of force, a revenge that is quick and clean and outside the law. In Lusby's *Flashback,* McCadden kills the boyfriend/pimp of one of the mutilated victims, summarily shooting this nefarious character in a fairground in Tramore. Embedded in this frontier-style justice is a critique of the soft, effeminate legal system of the bureaucratic welfare state. Ingrid Black's detective laments the sentence of a violent sex offender: "He was now in Mountjoy doing a ten-year stretch, having pleaded temporary insanity, diminished responsibility, deprived childhood, you name it."[12] In *The Guards* (2004), Bruen's Jack Taylor snaps when interviewing Mr. Planter, a vile character: "Something in his smug expression, the contempt in his voice, got me. I was up and smacking him across the face. I pulled him to his feet and he spat at me. I threw him from me, and his head came down heavily on the coffee table."[13] When this outburst turns out to have killed Planter, Taylor expresses no remorse—nor are we encouraged to feel any. The detective's form of outlaw justice and morality often lands him on the margins of society. He comes from and identifies with the working class. In noir, there is more to the plot than solving the case: what the detective uncovers is large-scale unfairness, the result of an unbridled, unchecked economy, and his mission is not only to bring a criminal to justice but, in some small measure, to right this larger wrong. It is eerily predictive, and perhaps a function of literature itself, that it is in the moral undercurrents of these novels that we see the economic crisis of today playing out. Although the detective in classic noir is afflicted with a nagging, fatalistic gloom, he helps those within his reach, often represented by the widow. In Galway, when Jack Taylor wins on the horses, he redistributes his money to a few homeless men and a Romanian beggar. Being on the margins allows him to critique the mainstream, in this case, the Celtic Tiger. In Galway, new hotels and apartment blocks have sprung up unchecked, but Jack Taylor gets evicted, and the only unchanged pub in the city, a pub that serves as his noir-style office, is about to be transformed into a "low-fat karaoke" bar. Our hero turns a cynical eye to progress, and this may be an obvious critique, but these novels, despite their low literary standing, serve this purpose with more prescience than most economists, politicians, and experts, just as Raymond Chandler highlighted the excesses of L.A.

If, in American noir, much of the white-hot judgment was directed at the sexually dangerous femme fatale, in Irish noir the moral hatred is reserved for the nouveau riche. In Allen's *Last to*

Know, Mugsy Mooney's wife is the symbol of the brashness associated with tacky striving for a place beyond one's "natural" class position. She wears tight animal prints, decorates her home with gauche velvet sofas, and she gets hers in the end: she is abandoned and demoted back to Finglas, a working-class project, where she clearly belonged all along. This is a clear (and conservative) literary move, one that showcases a backward-looking wish for the putative social clarity of earlier times as an antidote to the confusion of today.

The urban world of classic noir is fast-paced. The fragmented, disorganized city becomes the stage across which the detective races, through upscale neighborhoods, downtown bars, shady docklands, and the sprawling suburban margins; the noir detective never seems to sleep. Ireland, over the past decade, has changed physically almost beyond recognition; this newly unknowable landscape lends itself perfectly to the plot-driven tension of Irish noir. The detective is a sort of sociological tour guide, mapping and connecting the varied fragments and helping a middle-class reader understand his or her changing city, while maintaining its titillating glamour and danger. Whereas Chandler and Dashiell Hammett solve their cases against a boozy backdrop of whiskey and bourbon, the frenetic worlds of Deborah Parker, Jack Taylor, and Carl McCadden are fueled by cocaine. Certainly these Irish characters are not immune to the noir trope of alcohol, but their pace is more reflective of the overworked denizen of the Celtic Tiger, always on the run, forever zooming between obligations. And, if action is the metaphor that informs these novels, there is another, more concrete way in which they fit the new flavor of the Celtic Tiger. These thrillers are mass-marketed, sold at airports and railway stations, geared toward readers on the move, with little time for the more complicated nuances and psychologies of the high literature of their contemporaries such as William Trevor and John Banville. What strikes the reader first upon picking up one of these volumes is the elephantine size of the type—they look like I Can Read! books for adults. They are displayed facing outward, showcasing the terse titles and dark, gloomy images that grace their sensationalist covers. Readers know the plots of formula fiction in advance, so all that is required is to turn the pages and await the climax. These Irish noir novels strike a chord because they legitimate and attempt to organize chaos, while offering a speedy, easily manageable thrill in three hundred quick pages.

American noir offered a dark mirror to society. In the late 1920s and during the 1930s, the hard-boiled fiction of Chandler and Hammett captured a mood of betrayal, disillusionment, and gritty determination. Critics have read the alienation and existentialism of 1940s and 1950s film noir as a product of the trauma of World War II, the ending of American isolationism, impending McCarthyism and the red scare, and the emergence of the atomic age. Perhaps the defining trope that gives vent to all of these frustrations and fears is violence. Classic noir is physically brutal, and the sexually dangerous, threatening woman bears the brunt of male anger. In today's Irish thriller, women are again the victims of violence—a violence that is both more graphic and less ambivalent than its predecessor. Female victims in today's Irish noir novels are, across the board, both less threatening and more imperiled than those of sixty years ago. In each of the novels here discussed, the victims of violence— that is, the victims of Irish society—are prostitutes.

In high modernism, in the works of Walter Benjamin, Charles Baudelaire, and others, the figure of the prostitute typifies capitalism. The prostitute is an alienated body, the ultimate commodity, debased and without options in a brutal marketplace. It is no surprise, then, that Irish noir would appropriate this trope, projecting onto the mutilated body the fears of random violence and economic collapse. The violence in Irish noir, as in American noir, is titillating and melodramatic. The description of many of the murders—with an ironic nod to the shocking specificity of American postmodern entertainment, from *Pulp Fiction* to *CSI: Miami*—is exaggerated and more detailed than anything Irish literature has ever seen. In Lusby's *Flashback,* the victim could not be identified because her face had been bludgeoned repeatedly.

In Ireland today, violence continues to be on the rise: car crashes and road collisions reflect increased speed and affluence; turf wars and gangland murders over the drugs trade dominate headlines; random attacks on weekend nights in city streets are more common than ever, fueled once by a buoyant economy and a twenty-something generation with time to kill and money to spend, but fueled now, perhaps, by anger and fear. The more excessive and graphic the sexual brutality in these new novels, the more dramatic and satisfying the reward at the end, when the evildoers are brought to justice, the hero solves the case, and the women who survive emerge wounded but morally and materially victorious. These novels symbolically remake real violence, offering a mixture of palliation—crimes are solved, justice served—and titillation, and, through the figure of the noir detective, a certain existential resignation toward moral chaos and cultural uncertainty.

The similarity and popularity of these novels, as well as their transposition onto the Irish landscape, bring to mind a question posed by Angela Carter: what happens when literature becomes pure commodity? In this case, we are forced to acknowledge what perhaps has always been true but is now exaggerated: that national culture is not immutable, and that it exists within media images that come from elsewhere; that what is Irish is no longer what we thought of as a proud, specific, national tradition; that globalization makes us both more savvy and more similar and allows the mass marketing of Irishness. "What is exposed here," Carter says, "is the

notion that we are unique, that our literary history and quality of
production is unique, and that that uniqueness is tied to our history
and culture."[14] Cormac Millar, author of the contemporary thriller
An Irish Solution (2004), echoes Carter's point, in answering a question of this author about why he named his detective Seamus Joyce:
"We all live secondhand lives, parodying the archetypes of old literature."[15] Indeed, these noir thrillers may be the cultural equivalent
of the Celtic Tiger—itself a secondhand economy, dependent upon
multinationals, European directives, and American popular culture.

Noir has proven a persistent and popular genre. Neo-noir, from
Blade Runner to *Mullholland Drive* and *Se7en,* updates the original
theme of urban decay. Ireland before the Celtic Tiger did not have a
vast tradition of thrillers and crime novels, but the elements were
always there in latent form. Liam O'Flaherty's novel, *The Informer*
(1925), is explicitly cinematic, was written with an eye for Hollywood, and drew upon the techniques and themes of Weimar literary
expressionism: secret political organizations and the mysterious
cities that give them refuge.[16] The Troubles in Northern Ireland also
spawned a wave of noir novels, most notably Eoin McNamee's
Resurrection Man (2004). Here the context was Belfast, a great
industrial city, now rusting from neglect but overlaid with sophisti-
cated military surveillance technology. Belfast was an ideal landscape for tough guys embroiled in violence, chase, and psychological
terror.[17] Dublin itself, of course, has the clichéd literary history of
poetry rising from its sordid, grimy streets. The Dublin of the Celtic
Tiger brought this nostalgic industrial past together with a global,
cosmopolitan sheen, one that probably won't stand the test of time
and economic hardship but that was evidenced by gentrified tourist
districts, faux Georgian apartments, and a new burst of historical
preservation. Although this current outpouring of fiction may never
achieve high literary status, these novels cannot be dismissed as

trash, despite their questionable quality, convoluted plots, and over-the-top violence. They grapple with all of the issues on the minds of their readers, both during the years of the Celtic Tiger and now, in the midst of its collapse: a rapid urbanization and its attendant decline, shoddy construction, and half-finished projects; the changing shape of the family, and, perhaps for the first time in Ireland, a large immigrant population at a time of economic insecurity and cultural retrenchment; the perils of the putative end of sexual repression; increased levels of crime, to which are about to be added yet more poverty; and, in a more general way, fear, insecurity, threatened masculinity, and the collapsing structure of religion. Indeed, Celtic noir and its purveyors are as self-conscious about their own merits as about the merits of contemporary Irish culture.

NOTES

1. Jim Lusby, *Flashback* (London: Orion Books, 2001), 8.

2. Declan Kiberd, *The Irish Writer and the World* (Cambridge: Cambridge University Press, 2005), 286, 287.

3. Dozens of Irish potboiler thrillers have emerged over the last decade and a half. Declan Burke is the author of two hardboiled crime novels, *Eight-Ball Boogie* (2003) and *The Big O* (2007), both set in Sligo. Brian McGilloway's tough-cop character, Benedict Devlin, works the beat along the border between the Irish Republic and Northern Ireland, in *Borderlands* (2008) and *Bleed a River Deep* (2009). John Brady, an Irish writer based in Canada, locates his Inspector Matt Minogue series, including *Kaddish in Dublin* (2002) and *Wonderland* (2003), in Dublin's underworld of gangsters, migrants, corrupt politicians, and radical nationalists. The genre seems to lend itself to endless mutations. Eilis Ni Dhuibhne writes postmodern violence and snappy dialogue into an Irish-language mystery, *Dunmharu sa Daingean* (Murder in Dingle) (2000). Julie Parsons, a New Zealand-born writer, has produced five psychological thrillers between 1998 and 2005, and has had perhaps the most international success. Her books have been translated into seventeen languages. A recent issue of *Mystery Readers Journal—no.* 24 (Summer 2008), "Irish Mysteries"—contains interviews with over forty contemporary crime writers. *Dublin Noir,* a collection edited by Ken Bruen, appeared in 2006. A comprehensive list of contemporary Irish crime and hardboiled fiction can be found at: http://www.cormacmillar.com/Link-IrishCrimeWriters.html

4. Veronica Guerin was an Irish crime reporter who was murdered by drug dealers on June 26, 1996.

5. Sean Moncrieff, *Dublin* (London: Doubleday, 2001).

6. Cormac Miller, *An Irish Solution* (Dublin: Penguin Ireland, 2004).

7. "Old Emigrant Trail Beckons New Generation," *Irish Times*, sports section, May 9, 2009, p. 6.

8. "Disillusioned Diaspora Reflect on the Celtic Tiger's Downfall" and "Misery of the Returned Emigrant," *Irish Times*, February 13, 2009, p. 16.

9. Ingrid Black, *The Dead* (New York: St. Martin's Minotaur, 2004), 3.

10. Lusby, *Flashback,* 116.

11. Liz Allen, *The Last to Know* (London: Hodder and Stoughton, 2004).

12. Lusby, *Flashback,* 47.

13. Ken Bruen, *The Guards* (New York: St. Martin's Minotaur, 2001), 8.

14. Quoted in Kathy Cremin, "The Dispersed and Dismissed: The World of Irish Women's Best-Sellers," *Critical Survey* 15 (2003), 74.

15. Cormac O'Cuilleanain, "A Question about Seamus Joyce," email to the author, April 4, 2006.

16. Liam O'Flaherty, *The Informer* (Dublin: Wolfhound Press, 2008).

17. Eoin McNamee, *Resurrection Man* (London: Faber and Faber, 2004).

IMAGINING AND REIMAGINING A PROMISED LAND

THE GANGSTER GENRE AND HARLEM'S MYTHIC PAST, PRESENT, AND FUTURE

Paula J. Massood

In the opening scene of Ridley Scott's *American Gangster* (2007), crime boss Ellsworth "Bumpy" Johnson takes his protégé, Frank Lucas, to a newly opened big-box electronics store on 125th Street. Johnson uses the occasion to bemoan the changes in the community that he believes have resulted in the diminishment of the area's character. Shortly after his condemnation of chain stores and franchises, Johnson collapses and dies of a heart attack. Through its sympathetic presentation of the elderly Johnson, the scene suggests that Harlem gangsters of the past were gentlemen, and that the neighborhood, despite the presence of drugs and crime, was a community. But *American Gangster* is a story about Frank Lucas's rise and fall, not Bumpy Johnson's career, so this moment seems out of time and place. Indeed, despite its obsessive attention to period detail from the seventies, the film's apocryphal anti–big box message is more in keeping with twenty-first-century laments about Harlem's gentrification than it is about either Lucas or Johnson. And this is where the film becomes schizophrenic; *American Gangster* evokes the present even while located in two different pasts, the seventies and the thirties.

This schizophrenia is not limited to *American Gangster* in particular, or more generally to recent films set in Harlem. Nor are contemporary laments about current economic and political conditions in the neighborhood anything new; for example, the now-mythic Harlem of the Harlem Renaissance years was the by-product of overdevelopment, and concerns about overpriced real estate and the dearth of black property ownership extend back to the early twentieth-century when the area first became an African American neighborhood. But what is crucial here is to recognize the way in which *American Gangster,* like many films set in Harlem, mobilizes historical moments, particularly from the twenties and thirties, to grapple with the contemporary status of the neighborhood. More broadly, such historical references, refractions, and revisions can be understood as part of a continuing struggle to define what it means, and has meant, to be African American in the twentieth and twenty-first centuries.

This essay focuses on a selection of gangster films set in Harlem and made at different moments—the thirties, the seventies, and more recently—that share similar themes. First, many films focus on the figure of the black gangster or criminal, thus guaranteeing generic familiarity and box office appeal to a cross-section of viewers. More important, the black gangster references two enduring African American legacies: the urban trickster and the race man. Although seemingly contradictory, both characters represent forms of rebellion in the face of white power structures, and the popularity of black gangster films is often as much political as aesthetic. Second, many recent films incorporate symbols of Harlem's past—what John L. Jackson Jr. has called a "was-ness" that "tethers [the neighborhood] to another time altogether"—to explore the contemporary state of the nation's symbolic black center. This "other" time is often identified as the years associated with the Harlem Renaissance, when "Harlem was in vogue."[1] That this strategy has most recently been employed during a period of massive redevelopment in Harlem cannot be overlooked, and will be addressed here later.

BLACK GANGSTERS IN EARLY SOUND CINEMA

In the early thirties, Hollywood released a series of popular gangster films, including *Little Caesar* (Mervyn LeRoy, 1930), *The Public Enemy* (William A. Wellman, 1931), and *Scarface* (Howard Hawks, 1932). These films are considered the classics of the genre. Produced early in the sound era, they were products of a post-Crash, reform-minded society focused on the salvation of individuals involved in Prohibition-era "alternative economies" such as bootlegging, gambling, and racketeering. The gangster was drawn from contemporary headlines, and many films loosely followed the life stories of larger-than-life criminal figures such as Al Capone and John Dillinger, thus offering a "complicated interweaving of popular culture and social realities."[2] Particular cinematic aesthetics, aided by cinema's newest technology, sound, supported this interweaving: urban settings, location shooting, and the sounds of the city (vernacular speech, automobiles, sirens, horns, gunfire).

Although Hollywood gangster films neither featured black performers nor acknowledged a black urban presence, race film companies—production companies making films with black performers for black audiences—incorporated many of their conventions into black gangster films in the following years. During the twenties, the majority of race films were melodramas in which place was less important than narratives of racial uplift. This practice changed in the thirties with the independents' shift into genre production, making musicals, Westerns, and gangster films to compete against Hollywood films. As a city-based genre, the gangster film often was situated in an identifiable urban space, most often Chicago or New York. Black gangster films were, as well, though often much more explicitly by calling out their settings in their titles: for example, *Harlem Is Heaven* (1932), *Murder in Harlem* (1935), *Dark Manhattan* (1937), *Moon Over Harlem* (1939), and *Paradise in Harlem* (1939). This allusion to one of black America's most well-known spaces can be interpreted as an attempt to capitalize on Harlem's vogue among audience members (many of whom were urban dwellers), and as an acknowledgment of the area's transformative potential. Gangster films, with their focus on a protagonist's rise through the ranks of organized crime, presented an inseparable, and logical, relationship between urban space and character.

By the mid-thirties, Harlem was the primary location for black gangster films, the neighborhood serving as a shorthand signifier for African American modernity and possibility as a whole.[3] A few films were produced earlier in the decade; however, the majority of black gangster films did not appear until later, with the release of a group of mostly gangster and crime films made by Ralph Cooper and other West Coast filmmakers.[4] The first film in this cluster, Cooper's 1937 *Dark Manhattan,* is also the first true black gangster film, in that its focus on a small-time gangster rising through the ranks of organized crime adheres to the narrative conventions of earlier Hollywood films.[5] Despite these similarities, *Dark Manhattan* is a good example of the ways in which race film producers self-consciously adapted genre to address the specific experiences of their African American audiences.

Dark Manhattan follows a simple narrative: a low-level gangster named Curly Thorpe becomes the trusted right-hand man to L. B. Lee, an influential numbers king in Harlem. Lee, despite his illegal activities, is a model businessman and, perhaps more important, a race man who brings jobs and opportunity to the community. Curly is from the wrong side of the tracks—the "jungle," a neighborhood in downtown Manhattan—and his desire to climb the ladder to success, like many gangsters,' is fueled by greed and eventually stymied by hubris. His downfall is the result of his overreaching: he moves too fast and he alienates too many people along the way.

In its exposition of the specifics of black organized crime, *Dark Manhattan* utilizes and yet breaks with gangster film conventions. Historian David E. Ruth argues that in the late twenties and early thirties one of the most significant developments in Hollywood gangster films involved the presentation of the gangster's clothing and work environment. Early in the twenties, gangsters were (often ethnic) outsiders marked by a disheveled appearance, "garish cheap clothes," and surroundings that included "rough subterranean rooms … dirty, raucous saloons, and … dockyards and congested tenement districts." Later in the decade, however, gangsters began being depicted as "nattily dressed, office-using businessmen. Pleasant-featured, they wore three-piece suits, ties, hats, and watch-chains—a stylish version of standard middle-class business attire."[6] By the thirties, the gangster was a businessman, and criminal syndicates (formerly gangs) were structured as corporations.

Dark Manhattan follows these recently established conventions in many ways. L. B. Lee's operation is run as if it were a legitimate business, and L. B. himself is a staid, middle-aged businessman whose understated suits and well-appointed offices (populated by secretaries and a variety of clerks) barely suggest his true business dealings. Where the film breaks with Ruth's formula, however, is in

L. B.'s business: the numbers racket. Unlike Hollywood gangster films from the decade, which detailed the activities of bootleggers and racketeers, *Dark Manhattan* focuses on an activity that was "an integral part of the urban black experience and was understood more as a 'business' than racket." Numbers bankers "held special significance for their urban black community. . . . [and] were revered as proficient operators of a black-owned business in which all citizens had a stake."[7] They were, according to poet and writer Claude McKay, in *Harlem Glory: A Fragment of Aframerican Life,* "mystery men with a tremendous amount of respect, power, and money."[8] The film recognizes that the numbers racket is illegal, and yet its presentation of L. B. and other numbers bankers acknowledges their privileged position in the African American community. The illegal status of the numbers racket only becomes a problem through Curly's churlish and aggressive—that is, not businesslike—behavior.

When the elder L. B. becomes ill, Curly has an opportunity to take over the business. Although L. B. may be "the biggest numbers banker in Harlem," he is not the only one, and his young apprentice learns that he must answer to more than one boss. Curly doubles L. B.'s earnings, but he does so at the expense of other bankers, all of whom are bonded through their membership in the bankers' "association." The association is presented as a legitimate business organization and functions as "a metaphor for African American solidarity as a whole and as a reference to the history of black social movements [in general and] of the race man in particular."[9] This interpretation is not an exaggeration since, at this point, one of the most well-known numbers kings in Harlem was Casper Holstein, a West Indian by birth who had been involved in the numbers since the twenties. Holstein was a tremendously successful numbers banker who used much of his earnings to pursue philanthropic causes in Harlem and the West Indies, his two homes. He also was an important patron of the arts during the Harlem Renaissance, funding a number of the awards given by *Opportunity: The Journal of Negro Life*, and describing himself in the same magazine as "a firm and enthusiastic believer in the creative genius of the Negro race."[10] It is clear that L. B. Lee's appearance and behavior is meant to loosely and positively reference such figures as Holstein, who would have been widely known at this time.[11]

The film's acknowledgment of actual personalities and current social and political issues is an example of the way in which early black gangster films, though considered by many to be "impoverished emulations of dominant cinema," dialogued with contemporary African American urban life and contemporary African American representation. Like Oscar Micheaux and other earlier producers of silent uplift films, Cooper was concerned with making pictures that, he claimed, "glorified blacks,"[12] and *Dark Manhattan* is dedicated to "the memories of R. B. Harrison, Bert Williams, Florence Mills and all of the pioneer Negro actors who by their many sacrifices made this presentation possible."[13] The film's neutral stance on the numbers racket, L. B.'s genteel characterization, and Curly's come-uppance suggest that the film's "glorification" of blacks might not exactly fit the description of black achievement as articulated by W.E.B. Du Bois, but it acknowledged both the importance of black economic self-determination and the limited opportunities available for many black urbanites, especially during the Depression years. In this way, *Dark Manhattan*'s message was very much in keeping with the goals of uplift: African American success comes through hard work and solidarity, not through individual greed. A similar set of criteria echoes in Bumpy Johnson's words in *American Gangster*.

The Gangster in Blaxploitation Film

Most blaxploitation films—action films featuring black heroes and made to exploit the African American urban market—are not considered gangster films in the conventional sense; however, they do share many similarities with those earlier films, including an often sympathetic underworld protagonist, an urban setting, and a self-conscious relationship to social and political context. Blaxploitation films, like many of the Hollywood gangster revisions from the same time (including *Bonnie and Clyde* and *The Honeymoon Killers*), also referenced actual criminal personalities, particularly figures like Bumpy Johnson, Frank Lucas, and assorted other Harlem gangsters, drug dealers, and pimps. For example, films like *Shaft* (Gordon Parks Sr., 1971) and *Black Caesar* (Larry Cohen, 1973) referenced Johnson either by name or by legend. This, coupled with their low budget formal techniques, including location shooting, handheld camera, and the sounds of the street, provided the films with a sense of immediacy greater than that of the black gangster films from the thirties. For one thing, the earlier films were mostly produced on the West Coast and rarely included actual location shots of Harlem because it was cost-prohibitive to send a film crew to the East Coast. In the later films, Harlem's streets are used extensively and reflect changes in camera and sound technology that allowed more flexibility and economy in shooting on location. The meaning of the location is similar, however: Harlem provides the setting for a modern, politically engaged African American identity.

Blaxploitation films, like their predecessors, also consciously adapted genre to the experiences of their audiences, many of whom would have been familiar with Harlem's troubled urbanscape from the numerous television newscasts and special reports analyzing the area over the previous decade. For example, Harlem experienced a number of violent uprisings in the sixties, including a riot in 1964 that resulted in over one hundred injuries and one death, and scattered instances of violence in 1968 following the assassination of Martin Luther King Jr. Such instances of civil unrest were well documented in print and broadcast media, and were beamed into televisions across the world. This, coupled with newscasts such as "CBS Reports: The Harlem Temper," which was broadcast in 1963, and "New York Illustrated: A Block in Harlem," offered by WNBC in 1969, suggests a mass market focus on the neighborhood's myriad problems, including high rates of crime, joblessness, drug use, and illness.[14]

During this time, the Italians controlled Harlem's highly profitable drug business. It was also run by Frank Lucas, first in association with Johnson and then on his own. When Lucas came to Harlem in the late forties, he met Johnson and worked for him in some capacity (as driver, as bodyguard, as enforcer) until the latter's death in 1968.[15] By the early seventies, Lucas was a neighborhood legend, and was perhaps best known for breaking the grip of the Italian mob on the neighborhood's heroin business by working directly with sources in Southeast Asia. He was just as famous for his often unpredictable violence and his sartorial flamboyance (he was fond of mink and chinchilla hats and coats), the latter underscored by his self-inscribed nickname of Superfly. (In fact, American Gangster's working title was The Return of Superfly.) Unlike the more cerebral and understated figures of Casper Holstein and Bumpy Johnson— the latter of whom Lucas remembers as "a gentleman among gentleman, a king among kings, a killer among killers"—Lucas was larger than life, and no gentleman.[16] In effect, he was a later, nonfiction iteration of Curly Thorpe.

Blaxploitation films, especially those set in Harlem, often "blurred the line between the diegetic and the extradiegetic, forming

a complex dialogue between real and fictional urban landscapes"
and characters.[17] Nowhere is this more evident than in Gordon
Parks Jr.'s *Super Fly* (1972). Although it is unclear which may have
come first, Lucas's nickname or the film, the latter's title suggests the
dissolution of the line between fictional and nonfictional worlds, by
calling out actual Harlem personalities. The film narrates the story
of a mid-level Harlem drug dealer named Priest who wants to make
one more deal before getting out of the game. Unfortunately, neither Priest's partner nor his white associates are happy with his decision, and the narrative is filled with intrigue, double-crosses, drug
use, and violence. By the end of the film, however, Priest outwits his
pursuers and escapes the city, a happy ending compared to Curly's
demise at the hands, and guns, of the police.[18] This resolution is a
further change from earlier black gangster films, which tended to
voice "New Negro" optimism about the city's unlimited possibilities
even during the Depression. By the early seventies, the gangster, a
product of the city, tries to escape its streets.

Super Fly is not a biopic, yet it draws connections between
Lucas's and Priest's appearances and fights for independence and
self-determination, especially from organized crime and from the
police, the two controlling forces in the community. With its
discourses on self-determination and white corruption, *Super Fly*
appealed to audiences still reeling from the assassinations of Martin
Luther King Jr., Malcolm X, and Robert Kennedy and the string of
urban rebellions in the late-sixties, by articulating a more empow-
ered form of black pride, one that was taking root in black communities nationwide and was especially popular in neighborhoods like
Harlem, which had been decimated by years of poverty, crime, and
an overall governmental abandonment.[19] Yet Priest, like Lucas, is
not a rebel. In fact, in one scene he even rejects working with a militant group because he doesn't like their tactics (which don't include

"killing whitey").[20] Rather, his motivations for breaking with the drug trade are never articulated beyond his growing fatigue with what he's doing and his realization that others (whites) control him. Even so, Priest's appeal to audiences, especially urban, African American audiences, was that he fought the system and got away with the money.

In this latter element, the film also refigures the gangster genre. In the past, the protagonist would have paid for his sins, usually through death or incarceration. By the seventies, however, gangster protagonists survived, a result of the dissolution of the Motion Picture Production Code, the proscriptive list of acceptable content that the industry had used to regulate itself (to avoid government censorship) since the early thirties.[21] Yet, even though the films were popular, by 1975 blaxploitation production decreased, the combined victim of political and social pressures and the industry's new interest in blockbuster production. The same year, though entirely by coincidence, Frank Lucas was arrested for drug trafficking, starting a string of arrests and trials that eventually resulted in "Superfly's" serving a total of nine years in prison on various charges.

Lucas was paroled in 1991, the same year that John Singleton's *Boyz n the Hood*, Matty Rich's *Straight Out of Brooklyn*, and Mario Van Peebles's *New Jack City* were released (closely following the work of directors Spike Lee, Robert Townsend, and Reginald Hudlin in the mid-to-late eighties). The films, often called "hood" or "ghetto action" films, are coming-of-age tales set in inner-city neighborhoods in South Central Los Angeles and New York's Brooklyn.[22] As before, many directors were drawn to the gangster genre; however, the gangster had morphed into the "gangsta," a young, urban criminal with nothing much to lose.[23] And, though Brooklyn appeared much more frequently than Harlem, reflecting larger demographic shifts in New York, a number of films were set

in the Harlem neighborhood during this time. A few titles, like those
of decades before, call out the area, thus capitalizing on Harlem's
storied status as *the* African American neighborhood. But, in a
change from earlier films that used the name as a sign of modernity,
films like *Harlem Nights* (Eddie Murphy, 1989), *A Rage in Harlem*
(Bill Duke, 1991), and *Hoodlum* (Bill Duke, 1997), are set in the past,
revisiting the Harlem Renaissance. The effect is to contribute to that
period's mythology as the most significant moment in the neighborhood's, and perhaps in modern African American, history by
suggesting the sense of "was-ness" mentioned earlier. In doing so,
they present African American politics as historical rather than contemporary. Finally, they reconfigure ongoing debates about the gentrification of Harlem by refracting the present through the past.

THE REVAMPED BLACK GANGSTER FILM
OF THE NINETIES AND LATER

Bill Duke's *Hoodlum* returns to the numbers racket in Harlem of the
early thirties. The film focuses on the partnership between
Stephanie St. Clair, a French-born numbers queen, and Bumpy
Johnson during the early part of Johnson's career (prior to his
involvement in the heroin trade). St. Clair and Johnson are faced
with the attempted takeover of their business by Dutch Schultz, a
Jewish gangster who made most of his money in liquor during Prohibition and who is looking to diversify uptown. Initially, the Italians support Schultz, but they soon turn their backs on him for
drawing too much attention to the organization (in this way, they
function in a similar manner as the bankers' association in *Dark
Manhattan,* with Schultz's behavior similar to Curly's in the earlier
film). In the end, and after a number of double-crosses and colorful
shootouts, Johnson prevails (St. Clair spends most of the film in

prison) by orchestrating Schultz's assassination and freeing the neighborhood of Italian organized crime.

It is no surprise that *Hoodlum* takes liberties with Johnson's life story (along with St. Clair's and Schultz's). Although Schultz was gunned down in a mob-ordered hit for drawing too much attention to himself, Johnson was never an independent operator in Harlem. In fact, he served as the Italians' go-between and enforcer—its black face—until his death. Further, Johnson is presented as a Casper Holstein–like race man, a figure who provides the Depression-struck Harlemites with much-needed cash and articulating discourses of empowerment and self-determination closer in tone to the Million Man March than to New Negro political strategies of the twenties and thirties. Johnson may have been known for his social conscience and philanthropy—earning him the moniker of the "Robin Hood of Harlem"[24]—but the film presents the gangster as a respectable business person who only reluctantly engages in violence and crime, a model more in keeping with a thirties gangster like L. B. Lee than with those of succeeding decades. (In comparison, Gordon Parks Sr.'s *Shaft*, from 1971, depicts Johnson as someone who has terrorized the neighborhood with his violence and drug dealing. Because of *Hoodlum*'s historical time frame, there is no acknowledgment of Johnson's involvement in the distribution of drugs over the next few decades.) By keeping to this nostalgic rendering of the neighborhood, the film, with its sepia tones and jazz- and blues-based soundtrack, alludes to a simpler, more perfect time before drugs replaced the numbers and the black outlaws considered in the best interests of the neighborhood.

The discussion of these changes should not be mistaken as a plea for cinematic verisimilitude. Rather, it is more to point out the ongoing links between the black gangster and the race man, a figure who succeeds in the only business open to him and who uses his ill-gotten gains to help his community. By the time *Hoodlum* was made in 1997, Harlem had lost much of its identity as a cohesive African American community, so it is no coincidence that films begin to appear reminding us of its glorious past. In a neighborhood still experiencing the effects of high unemployment, violent crime, and drugs (crack cocaine), and on the cusp of massive development, Johnson appears as a panacea for contemporary audiences, a cure-all for local, and perhaps national, ills. Also, what at first might seem cinematic wishful thinking becomes more interesting when compared to films like *Boyz n the Hood* and *Menace II Society,* the prevailing black gangster/gangsta films of the time, which often referenced early (white) gangster films yet misunderstood the way that the conventions of such films could be adapted for context. In this context, *Hoodlum* can be read as an object lesson on the outlaw's responsibility to the community and as a warning about the negative effects of outside interests in black neighborhoods.

American Gangster, made ten years after *Hoodlum,* makes no such heroic claims about the gangster. Frank Lucas, unlike Johnson, is no race man. According to Lucas's own account, "There wasn't gonna be no next Bumpy. Bumpy believed in that share-the-wealth. I was a different sonofabitch. I wanted all the money for myself."[25] The opening of this essay noted that the traces of an historical schizophrenia can be spotted in *American Gangster*'s opening scene. Johnson's harangue against large supermarkets, MacDonald's, and big-box electronics stores is a lament for the past, when, according to the elder gangster, there was "pride of ownership" and "personal service."[26] Johnson identifies the chain stores as "what's wrong with America," and by extension Harlem. This is ironic, coming from a drug dealer, even one with a philanthropic past. But Johnson's reference to a time before multinational corporations and globalization is even more interesting when one takes in to account that

Harlem, like many predominately black urban centers, was never really considered part of America (or not until, perhaps, Bill Clinton took up residency in the neighborhood in 2001).

The film transitions from such a critique, and instead uses Johnson's lament, "What right do they have cutting out the suppliers, the middlemen, buying direct, putting *Americans* out of work?" as a business model. Lucas takes Johnson's words as a lesson on circumventing his Italian heroin suppliers and going directly to the source in Southeast Asia. Later in the film, Lucas describes this strategy as his guarantee that no one will ever "own" him as the Italians owned Johnson. Ultimately, this discourse on self-determination, while in keeping with the message of economic independence expressed in the earlier films, suggests a shift from uplift versions of the self-effacing and community-minded black gangster to a new model of the American gangster as a global capitalist. In this model, the drug trade in Harlem ironically becomes part of an American business ethos in which global economics come to bear (often to negative effect) on local relationships.

WHERE IS HARLEM NOW?

The continuing nostalgia for Harlem past, as presented in contemporary film and advertised by the Langston Condominiums, the Lenox Condominiums, One Striver's Row, and other recent luxury condo developments in the neighborhood, suggests the capitalization of a mythical "Mecca of the New Negro" that references African American culture but is often more about real estate and global conglomerates such as Starbucks, Old Navy, and the Gap. Yet the use of gangster conventions to explore African American urban life, whether from the thirties, the seventies, or more recently, suggests something equally compelling. The making of legends out of murderers, pimps, dealers, and racketeers links, of course, to African American oral traditions of the trickster. But the films' discourses on uplift and economic independence illustrate the continuing battles between identity and capital being waged, sometimes violently, in Harlem. Denzel Washington may play Frank Lucas as a hero in *American Gangster,* but, in terms of economic self-determination, it's Casper Holstein, the only gangster who bought property in his own neighborhood, who may end up being the hero of this very American story. American gangster or not, even Lucas couldn't afford his neighborhood's new luxury condos.

ACKNOWLEDGMENTS

This essay is a distillation of more detailed arguments that appear in *Making a Promised Land: Harlem in Twentieth-Century Photography and Film* (Rutgers University Press, 2013).

NOTES

1. John L. Jackson Jr., *Harlemworld: Doing Race and Class in Contemporary Black America* (Chicago: University of Chicago Press, 2001), 21. See also David Levering Lewis, *When Harlem Was in Vogue* (New York: Penguin Books, 1997).

2. Jonathan Munby, *Public Enemies Public Heroes: Screening the Gangster from* Little Caesar *to* Touch of Evil (Chicago: University of Chicago Press, 1999), 67.

3. Paula J. Massood, *Black City Cinema: African American Urban Experiences in Film* (Philadelphia: Temple University Press, 2003), 61.

4. The Popkins, based in Hollywood, established Million Dollar Productions in 1937 and, with Ralph Cooper, specialized in gangster films, producing, according to Henry T. Sampson, some of the most "stylish black films" of the day (between 1937 and 1940). Henry T. Sampson, *Blacks in Black and White: A Source Book on Black Films,* 2nd. ed. (Lanham, Md.: Scarecrow Press, 1995), 222. The average Million Dollar film had a budget of $12,000 (20), a figure on the high end of an industry with budgets ranging from $3,000 to $20,000 (and with most on the lower end of this range), according to Jesse Zunser in "Harlem Goes Hollywood" [source NA, from *Dark Manhattan* clippings file, Billy Rose Theater Collection, New York Library for the Performing Arts].

5. *Dark Manhattan* was the brainchild of Cooper, its star, and his producing partner George Randol, who also served as the film's screenwriter. Cooper was an entertainer, most well known for his work as an actor, as a song-and-dance man, and as the emcee of the Apollo Theater's Amateur Night (which he founded in 1934). In the mid-thirties, he moved to Hollywood, and was initially contracted to choreograph routines and to appear opposite Shirley Temple in a number of films produced by 20th Century Fox. When this fell through, Cooper tried to interest the studios in making all-black films. Receiving no response, he joined with Randol to produce his own films. One of the benefits of Cooper's contract was that he trained at Fox's film school and thus had a working knowledge of film form and structure. George Randol was a veteran stage performer, having appeared on Broadway, for example in both the original production and the revival of Marc Connelly's *The Green Pastures*. The partners joined with Million Dollar Productions after running out of funds. The Popkins's production company helped finance and distribute *Dark Manhattan* and worked with Cooper on two more gangster films, *Bargain with Bullets* (1937) and *Gang War* (1939), and on a musical, *The Duke Is Tops* (1938), which also starred Lena Horne.

6. As David Ruth suggests in *Inventing the Public Enemy: The Gangster in American Culture, 1918–1934* (Chicago: University of Chicago Press, 1996), 41–42, many early gangster films resorted to determinist conclusions to explain protagonist's behavior. Such is not the case here. Although reference is made to his past, Curly is not punished for his origins. He is punished for not recognizing tradition.

7. Munby, *Public Enemies Public Heroes*, 274.

8. The numbers appear as a subject in a variety of novels, short stories, poems, and nonfiction works from this time. McKay himself would mention the subject in more than one publication. Munby mentions McKay's history of the numbers in *Harlem: Negro Metropolis* (1940). In *Harlem Glory: A Fragment of Aframerican Life* (published posthumously in 1990, but written around the same time as *Harlem: Negro Metropolis*), McKay offers a chapter-length description of the history and the structure of numbers. See *Harlem Glory: A Fragment of Aframerican Life* (Chicago: Charles H. Kerr, 1990), especially pages 12–15.

9. Massood, *Black City Cinema*, 64.

10. Quoted in Ron Chepesiuk, *Gangsters of Harlem: The Gritty Underworld of New York's Most Famous Neighborhood* (Fort Lee, N.J.: Barricade Books, 2007), 30. *Opportunity: A Journal of Negro Life* was published by the National Urban League from 1923 to 1949. Edited by scholar Charles S. Johnson, *Opportunity: The Journal of Negro Life* published pieces by many authors associated with the Harlem Renaissance.

11. Earlier in the decade, Holstein had been kidnapped, in a widely covered case, adding to his notoriety.

12. Quoted in Munby, *Public Enemies Public Heroes,* 272.

13. Ibid.

14. "New York Illustrated: A Block in Harlem" was an episode in a long-running public affairs program, narrated by Lee Wood and produced by WNBC-TV. The episode focused on a partnership between the City of New York and the Frederick W. Richmond Foundation to rehabilitate one block of 114th Street in Harlem. By the time that the episode aired, the abysmal state of Harlem's housing stock was already well known; for example, the 1960 Census found that only 51 percent of the neighborhood's housing units were sound, while "half are either 'deteriorating' or dilapidated.'" For more, see Alphonso Pinkney and Roger R. Woock Pinkney's *Poverty and Politics in Harlem: A Report of Project Uplift* (New Haven, Conn.: College and University Press, 1970), 29.

15. *American Gangster* fictionalized the circumstances of Johnson's death. He died on June 7, 1968, of a heart attack, while seated in a Harlem restaurant.

16. Quoted in Mark Jacobson, "The Return of Superfly," *New York Magazine,* August 7, 2000. http://nymag.com/nymetro/news/people/features/3649/ (accessed November 4, 2007).

17. Massood, *Black City Cinema,* 106.

18. A more recent film, *Sugar Hill* (Leon Ichaso, 1994), follows a similar plot about a Harlem drug dealer trying to escape the trade. Unlike *Super Fly,* it ends tragically with the death of the hero.

19. From Marcus Garvey's Universal Negro Improvement Association onward, Harlem had been the home to a variety of proactive political movements that supported a strategy of Black Nationalism over more assimilationist groups like the Urban League or the NAACP. By the early seventies, for example, the area had thriving arms of the Nation of Islam and the Black Panther Party.

20. This scene exemplifies the film's schizophrenic politics: the militants (as they are called in the credits), approach Priest and demand that he pay his due to the movement after having made so much money peddling drugs to the neighborhood. They want a donation to aid in their attempts to "build a new nation for black people." Priest's refusal is based on the fact that their plans don't include armed insurrection. In effect, the militants aren't militant enough.

21. The Motion Picture Production Code lasted until the late sixties (though it was systematically dismantled over the course of the decade), and was replaced by the ratings system that remains (with slight changes) in place today. The Production Code prescribed acceptable content for Hollywood films; for example, scenes of crimes being committed could not be shown unless the criminal was punished. The Production Code also prohibited scenes of miscegenation. Scholars have argued that when the code was dismantled in the sixties, American films quickly began including, and sometimes

highlighting, previously forbidden content, such as violence, sex, and nudity. The results could be seen in blaxploitation films, which often feature explicit sex scenes between the races, particularly sex between black men and white women (*Shaft* and *Super Fly* are two examples).

22. See Massood, *Black City Cinema,* for the former, and Watkins, "Ghetto Reelness: Hollywood Film Production, Black Popular Culture, and the Ghetto Action Film Cycle," in *Genre and Hollywood,* ed. Steve Neale (London: BFI Publishing, 2002), for the latter.

23. For more on this, see Todd Boyd, *Am I Black Enough for You?: Popular Culture from the 'Hood and Beyond* (Bloomington: Indiana University Press, 1997), and S. Craig Watkins, *Representing: Hip Hop Culture and the Production of Black Cinema* (Chicago: University of Chicago Press, 1999).

24. Chepesiuk, *Gangsters of Harlem,* 92–95.

25. Quoted in Jacobson, *New York Magazine.*

26. Dialogue taken from Steven Zaillian, *American Gangster,* final shooting script. http://www.simplyscripts.com/oscar80.html (accessed July 27, 2006).

NOTES ON
CONTRIBUTORS

ACKBAR ABBAS is a professor of comparative literature at the University of California, Irvine. Previously he was chair of comparative literature at the University of Hong Kong (HKU) and also codirector of the Centre for the Study of Globalization and Cultures at HKU. His research interests include globalization, Hong Kong and Chinese culture, architecture, cinema, postcolonialism, and critical theory. His books include *Hong Kong: Culture and the Politics of Disappearance* (1997) and *Internationalizing Cultural Studies,* coedited with John Erni (2005). He currently serves as a contributing editor to *Public Culture.*

SHERRY AHRENTZEN is the Shimberg Professor of Housing Studies at the University of Florida, and formerly was associate director of the Stardust Center for Affordable Homes and the Family at Arizona State University. Her research—focusing on sustainable residential practices that foster the physical, social, and economic health of households—has been published extensively in journals, books, and magazines. The nature of her work is multidisciplinary and collaborative, and spans the housing studies spectrum from building construction and technology to interior and architectural design, from neighborhood development to community design.

ALFONSO IRACHETA is an architect and urban and regional planner. He is head of the Urban and Environmental Studies Program at El Colegio Mexiquense, Zinacantepec, Mexico, and president of the National Urban Land Congress, FOROPOLIS, and Centro EURE in Mexico. Author of five books and coeditor of fifteen, and author of more than fifty articles and book chapters, Iracheta has lectured internationally on urban issues. He is a member of the HS-NET (Human Settlement Network) Advisory Board of UN-Habitat.

ANDREW KINCAID is associate professor of English at the University of Wisconsin–Milwaukee. His book, *Postcolonial Dublin: Imperial Legacies and the Built Environment,* was published in 2006. His articles have appeared in *College Literature, Journal of Commonwealth and Postcolonial Studies,* and *Eire-Ireland.* Currently he is working on a study of Irish maritime modernity, as well as on an exploration of the connections among urban planning, port cities, and security.

LINDA KRAUSE is associate professor of architectural history and criticism in the Department of Architecture, and associate dean in the School of Architecture and Urban Planning, University of Wisconsin–Milwaukee. She also participates in the Buildings, Landscapes, Culture collaborative initiative with the History of Art Department at the University of Wisconsin–Madison. Her research and teaching areas include nineteenth- and twentieth-century architectural and urban design history, theory, and criticism. She has published articles on architectural and urban theory and coedited, with Patrice Petro, *Global Cities: Cinema, Architecture, and Urbanism in a Digital Age* (2003).

PAULA J. MASSOOD is professor of film studies in the Department of Film, Brooklyn College, CUNY, and on the doctoral faculty in the

Program in Theatre at the Graduate Center, CUNY. She is the author of *Black City Cinema: African American Urban Experiences in Film* (2003) and editor of *The Spike Lee Reader* (2008), and has served as the film and theater subject editor for the African American National Biography project. She is currently completing a monograph on film and photography in Harlem for Rutgers University Press.

LINDA MCCARTHY is an associate professor of geography at the University of Wisconsin–Milwaukee, a faculty member of its Urban Studies Program, and a certified planner. Her research activities focus on urban and regional economic development and planning in the United States, Western Europe, and China. Her recent work has been on regional cooperation, competition among localities for private-sector investment and jobs, the globalization of the economy, the automobile industry, and brownfield redevelopment. Her publications comprise scholarly articles, book chapters, agency reports, and books, including *The Geography of the World Economy* (2008) with Paul Knox and John Agnew, and *Urbanization* (2012) with Paul Knox.

CHARLES WALDHEIM is the John E. Irving Professor of Landscape Architecture and chair of the Department of Landscape Architecture at Harvard University's Graduate School of Design. His teaching and research examine the relationships between landscape and contemporary urbanism. Waldheim coined the term *landscape urbanism* to describe the recent emergence of landscape as a medium of urban order for the contemporary city. He has authored numerous articles and chapters on the topic, and edited *The Landscape Urbanism Reader* (2006). He is a licensed architect and principal of Urban Agency, a multidisciplinary consultancy in design and contemporary urbanism.

GEORGIA BUTINA WATSON is professor of urban design, head of the Department of Planning, and research director of Urban Design at Oxford Brookes University. Her professional expertise includes the study of, and consultancy work in, urban regeneration, place identity, community development, and sustainable cities. She has an extensive portfolio of urban regeneration consultancy projects in the United Kingdom and overseas. Watson has coauthored a number of books, including *Identity by Design* with Ian Bentley (2007) and *Designing Sustainable Cities in the Developing World* with Roger Zetter (2006).

MO ZELL is an associate professor of architecture at the University of Wisconsin–Milwaukee and cofounding principal of bauenstudio, an award-winning design and research firm located in Milwaukee, Wisconsin. Zell combines research, teaching, and design practice with the goal of integrating buildings with existing context, site, and situation to achieve place. She is the author of *The Architectural Drawing Course* (2008). Zell is a registered architect in Massachusetts.

INDEX

accessory dwelling unit (AUD),
52–53
affordable housing. *See* housing
affordability
agrarian urbanism, 5, 63–65, 71, 73;
reform, 20, 24n13
agricultural production, 63–64, 73
Agronica (Andrea Branzi), 5, 65,
71–74
Allen, Liz: *The Last to Know,*
124, 126
Allen, Stan, 72, 106
American Gangster (film), 9, 10n8;
as distinct from earlier uplift films,
141, 143; and economic self-
determination, 148–150, 152n15;
evoking the 1930s and 1970s, 136;
as indicative of changes in Harlem,
135
American Recovery and
Reinvestment Act (ARRA), 58
Amsterdam, social diversity and
housing subsidies, 55
Angell Town, U.K.: as case study for
planning and urban design, 83–84;
1970s housing development, 84–86;
redesign of, 88–93; spatial
segregation and socio-cultural
problems in, 86
Angell Town Community Project
(ATCP), 86–87, 89
animalia, 72

anticipation, as a characteristic of
contemporary Chinese cities,
111–112, 114
anti-poaching pacts, 33, 38
Apache Junction, AZ, 43
arbitrage, as a characteristic of
contemporary Chinese cities,
113–114
Archigram, 71
Architettura Radicale, Florence,
Italy, 71
Archizoom, Milan, Italy, and No-
Stop City, 71
Armour Institute of Technology, 69
ARRA (American Recovery and
Reinvestment Act), 58
Astronautics Corp. of America,
25–26, 38
ATCP (Angell Town Community
Project), 86–87, 89
AUD (accessory dwelling unit), 52–53
Aureli, Pier Vittorio, and
Stop-City, 72

Banville, John, 129
Barthes, Roland, 121
Baudelaire, Charles, 130
bauenstudio, 96–99, 102, 106
Bauhaus, 68
Beijing, Mandarin Oriental
Hotel, 119
Beijing Trilogy (films), 115

159

CPSIA information can be obtained at www.ICGtesting.com
Printed in the USA
BVOW032136211012

303445BV00001B/4/P